THE
TEA
BOOK

THE
TEA
BOOK

Linda Gaylard

DK UK
Project Editor Kathy Woolley
Project Art Editor Vicky Read
Managing Editor Dawn Henderson
Managing Art Editor Christine Keilty
Senior Jacket Creative Nicola Powling
Pre-Production Producer Dragana Puvacic
Producer Jen Scothern
Deputy Art Director Maxine Pedliham
Design Director Phil Ormerod
Publisher Peggy Vance

DK INDIA
Senior Editor Dorothy Kikon
Editors Seetha Natesh, Gopa Pincha
Art Editors Neha Wahi, Sourabh Challariya
Managing Editor Alicia Ingty
Managing Art Editor Navidita Thapa
DTP Designers Tarun Sharma,
  Syed Md. Farhan
Pre-production Manager Sunil Sharma

First published in Great Britain in 2015 by
Dorling Kindersley Limited, 80 Strand,
London WC2R 0RL

A NOTE ON THE MAPS: See page 224

A CIP catalogue record for this book
is available from The British Library
ISBN 978-0-2411-8228-4

Colour reproduction by AltaImage Ltd
Printed and bound in Hong Kong

All images © Dorling Kindersley Limited
For further information see: www.dkimages.com

A WORLD OF IDEAS:
SEE ALL THERE IS TO KNOW
www.dk.com

CONTENTS

FOREWORD

There are two questions that I am often asked when people learn that I am a tea sommelier: first, what is a tea sommelier? and second, how did I become so interested in tea?

I like to answer the second question first. While it might imply that there was an exact moment in time when I abandoned the tea bags and elected to follow the "true path of tea", this was not the case. Rather, there was a gradual introduction to loose-leaf tea that slowly and steadily changed my perspective. Through study, experience, travelling to places where tea originated, and learning from industry masters, I found myself immersed in the world of tea.

The nuances of other tea cultures were revealed layer by layer, as I came to understand their unique styles of tea and their traditions of preparation and serving. While formalities are to be respected with ceremonies and traditions, the modern approach to tea encourages fresh experiences such as tea mixology, cold infusions, lattés, and much more. I enjoy discovering new ways to experience tea, sometimes fusing the practices of one culture with those of another.

The first question still hangs in the air, and I hope that after answering the "how", the "what" begins to make sense. The tea sommelier has the challenging task of convincing tea drinkers that there is much more to tea than a mug and a tea bag. Beyond the bag there is mystery, history, travel, industry, culture, and ceremony: a whole new world to explore.

I want *The Tea Book* to be your entry into this vast and enticing universe. Whether you are new to loose leaves or know your oolong from your Pu'er, you will find something to interest you. I hope you will develop your own thirst for tea, and the adventures it will provide.

Linda Gaylard

WHAT IS TEA?

TODAY'S TEA LOVER

There is more high-quality loose-leaf tea available to us, and more infusion gadgets to prepare it, than ever before. This is creating a culture of tea followers with a thirst for knowledge and new tea experiences.

In the first half of the last century all of the tea that was consumed around the world was loose-leaf. As lifestyles changed, and convenience became more important than flavour and tradition, consumers were won over by the ease of preparing tea using a tea bag. Now, discerning tea drinkers are returning to loose-leaf tea, honing their tasting skills, and acquiring knowledge of a vast array of high-quality teas that they are able to prepare and drink in their homes as well as in restaurants and cafés. Curious consumers might want to discover more about global tea cultures, such as ancient tea ceremonies, or go online to connect with tea growers and sellers, tea specialists, and tea bloggers to share and accumulate information from the world of tea.

TEA ON THE HIGH STREET

An indication that this passion for tea is no passing fad is the increasing variety and availability of excellent quality tea. Walk into any supermarket and you will find a diverse selection of loose-leaf tea, as well as the convenient new take on the tea bag – the cleverly designed silk pyramid sachet filled with high-quality loose leaves, such as jasmine pearls, Chinese greens, and Silver Needle white tips. One doesn't have to travel very far along the high street to find a teashop that is well stocked with tea from the far corners of the globe. Cafés that previously served only coffee or generic black tea have cleared shelf space for specialty loose-leaf tea with the latest tea gadgets and knowledgeable staff to serve it. Improved tea lists are appearing on restaurant menus, and some "tea bars" are offering tea cocktails and tea cuisine. Unique and exotic teas are entering our everyday consciousness and all the signs tell us that this tea trend is continuing to grow.

With all this recent exposure to specialty and premium tea, a new breed of tea-lover is developing: a tea-lover that treks to countries of origin, studies tea customs, meets growers, and brings home rare Pu'er and little-known green teas to share with their tea-loving friends.

MIXOLOGY
More than just a mixer, the right tea can add layers of flavour and complexity to a cocktail.

JAPANESE GREEN
Green tea from Japan, such as this Sencha, is famous for its delicate sweetness and marine flavour.

Sweet iced tea has been consumed throughout North America for over a century.

WHAT'S NEW IN TEA?

People may have started drinking tea hundreds of years ago, but a resurgent interest in the drink has led to a thriving new tea scene, which takes the best teas, traditions, and rituals from around the world and makes them part of our everyday lives.

MUCH ADO ABOUT MATCHA

Matcha is trending among health-conscious tea drinkers. This green tea-leaf powder can be consumed in a shot glass for a morning jolt of caffeine and antioxidants, as a creamy latté, mixed with fruits and ready to drink from the chiller cabinet, or in baked goods such as shortbread and macarons.

TEA MIXOLOGY

Mixologists have found tea's rich and refreshing variety of flavours a delectable addition to their stock of ingredients for cocktails. "Teatinis", martinis made using tea, have arrived at upscale bars, and can be easily prepared at home, too.

DESSERT TEA

Just as mixologists are experimenting with cocktails, tea blenders are innovating with "dessert tea" (see pp62–63) – taking inspiration from the dessert menu and recreating those flavours in delicious tea concoctions made using fruit, chocolate, and spices.

FERMEN-TEA-TION

Kombucha, the fizzy and fermented tea with powerful probiotic properties, is popping up in shops, pre-bottled in multiple flavours, and in bars, as a cocktail ingredient, all around the world. Although readily available pre-bottled, it is fun to make at home (see p174).

GOURMET TREAT

Gracing the tables of high-end restaurants, tea is fast becoming a popular food ingredient. Why not try tea recipes such as Masala Chai scones, green tea salad dressing, and Lapsang Souchong meat rubs.

SPECIALTY TEAS ARE TAKING OVER MORE AND MORE SHELF SPACE IN THE SUPERMARKETS

GOOD HEALTH IN A CUP

Tea has long been consumed for its health properties, but the wealth of new research on tea is highlighting more health benefits than the original tea pioneers could ever have imagined. Green tea, with its "health halo", is now so popular that it is being grown in countries that didn't traditionally produce it, such as India and Sri Lanka, to keep up with world demand.

TEA ON THE GO

Ready-to-drink bottled tea is a great "grab and go" option, and is available in numerous shops, cafés, and vending machines on the high street. Available au naturel or with the addition of fruit, gelled coconut, and other interesting ingredients, bottled tea is becoming more popular than ever.

BUBBLE TEA

Colourful and tasty, bubble tea (see p192) has taken the world by storm since it first appeared in Taiwan in the 1980s. Everything about it, from the oversized straws used to drink the tea to the chewy tapioca boba (the bubbles at the bottom) bursting with flavour, makes it a fun experience.

BEST SERVED CHILLED

Extracting more natural sweetness than hot tea, and with less caffeine, cold infusion (see pp58–59), or infusing leaves using cold water, is a growing trend. There is a wide variety of equipment available, from easy-to-use infusers to more elaborate teaware, to help you make and enjoy these chilled teas.

THE PLANT THAT CHANGED THE WORLD

Countless types of tea are produced and enjoyed globally, and although they might look and taste very different, they are all made from the leaves of the versatile evergreen plant, Camellia sinensis.

CAMELLIA SINENSIS

There are two main varieties of *Camellia sinensis*. The first, *Camellia sinensis* var. *sinensis,* produces teas with flavours ranging from bright and fresh to rich and malty. It is a small-leaved plant suited to a cool, misty climate, such as on the higher elevations of mountainous regions in China, Taiwan, and Japan. This variety can grow to a height of 6m (20ft) if left undisturbed. The second, *Camellia sinensis* var. *assamica,* is a larger-leaved plant that thrives in tropical regions, such as India, Sri Lanka, and Kenya. Its leaves can grow as long as 20cm (8in) and, in the wild, it can grow to a height of 15m (50ft). This variety produces teas with flavours ranging from mellow and grassy to brisk and malty.

CULTIVARS: THE CHARACTER OF A PLANT

One of the characteristics of the tea plant is its ability to adapt naturally to its ambient conditions, making it wholly suited to the region in which it is grown. Growers often build upon distinguishing traits of their tea plants by creating "cultivars", or cultivated varieties. They do this by selecting plants with distinct qualities, such as special flavour attributes or an ability to endure drought or repel insects.

As a result of human intervention, as well as natural occurrence, there are now more than 500 hybrids of tea plant. Some of these are bred exclusively for a specific type of tea, such as the Da Bai Hao cultivar for Silver Needle white tea, or Japanese Yabukita, the most popular cultivar in Japan.

TEA CULTIVATION
A typical terraced plantation on the slopes of the Cameron Highlands in Malaysia (above). *Camellia sinensis* var. *sinensis* (right) produces nuanced flavours because of its slow growth.

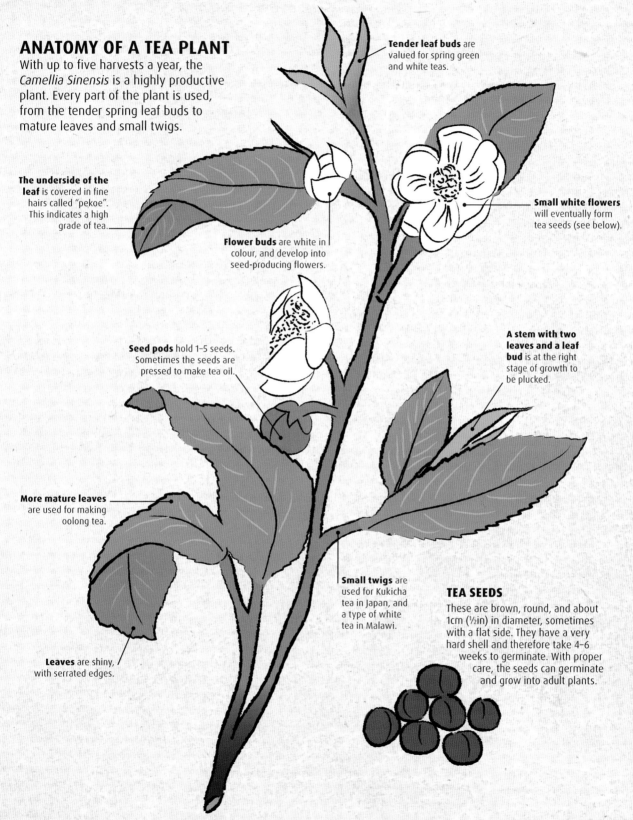

ANATOMY OF A TEA PLANT

With up to five harvests a year, the *Camellia Sinensis* is a highly productive plant. Every part of the plant is used, from the tender spring leaf buds to mature leaves and small twigs.

Tender leaf buds are valued for spring green and white teas.

The underside of the leaf is covered in fine hairs called "pekoe". This indicates a high grade of tea.

Flower buds are white in colour, and develop into seed-producing flowers.

Small white flowers will eventually form tea seeds (see below).

Seed pods hold 1–5 seeds. Sometimes the seeds are pressed to make tea oil.

A stem with two leaves and a leaf bud is at the right stage of growth to be plucked.

More mature leaves are used for making oolong tea.

Small twigs are used for Kukicha tea in Japan, and a type of white tea in Malawi.

Leaves are shiny, with serrated edges.

TEA SEEDS

These are brown, round, and about 1cm (½in) in diameter, sometimes with a flat side. They have a very hard shell and therefore take 4–6 weeks to germinate. With proper care, the seeds can germinate and grow into adult plants.

GROWTH AND HARVEST

The adult tea plant is hardy and can withstand a wide range of weather conditions, but it is slow to grow from seed. Tea growers, therefore, take special care of their young plants while they wait for the seeds to sprout and mature.

FROM SEED OR CLONE

The tea plant is grown for its foliage rather than its flowers or fruit (seeds). The ultimate aim is to have abundant new growth as often as possible throughout the growing season to ensure a healthy harvest. There are varying opinions on how to produce new plants successfully. Artisan growers often cultivate plants from seed because they believe that the adult plant will be stronger for having fought its way through the seed barrier and up through the ground. More often, however, tea is propagated from cuttings, which eventually grow into adult plants, called clonal plants. These are ready for harvest slightly sooner than seedlings, and their characteristics dependably represent those of the mother plant, so are a safer bet for many growers.

GROWING FROM SEED

It takes more than one year for a flower to seed. Flowers start to bud on the tea plant in summer, opening in early autumn. The seeds fall when the weather turns colder (October–January) and are gathered from the ground soon after. In China, they are collected in late autumn or early winter.

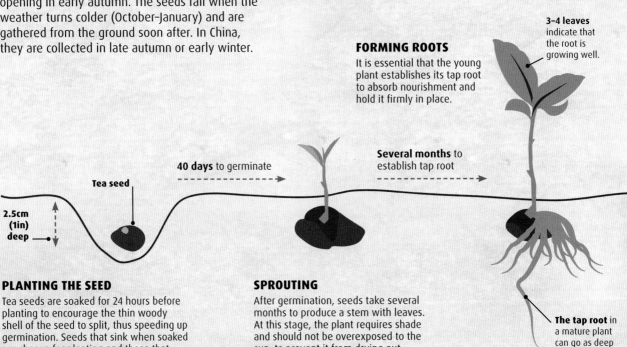

FORMING ROOTS
It is essential that the young plant establishes its tap root to absorb nourishment and hold it firmly in place.

3–4 leaves indicate that the root is growing well.

40 days to germinate

Several months to establish tap root

Tea seed

2.5cm (1in) deep

The tap root in a mature plant can go as deep as 6m (20ft).

PLANTING THE SEED
Tea seeds are soaked for 24 hours before planting to encourage the thin woody shell of the seed to split, thus speeding up germination. Seeds that sink when soaked are chosen for planting and those that float are discarded.

SPROUTING
After germination, seeds take several months to produce a stem with leaves. At this stage, the plant requires shade and should not be overexposed to the sun, to prevent it from drying out.

Single leaf

**Cutting, 2.5–5cm
(1–2in) long**

PROPAGATION FROM CUTTING

During the dormant, or dry, season, a cutting of 2.5–5cm (1–2in) with only one healthy leaf is taken from the middle portion of the primary shoot of the plant. (This is the shoot that grows directly out of the main trunk of the "mother plant".) The stem is cut diagonally, with a sharp knife, about 5mm (¼in) above and 2.5cm (1in) below the leaf, then planted in a pot. Cuttings should be kept out of direct sunlight and the leaf sprayed with water daily.

After 12–15 months, the cutting will have grown roots and is ready to be transferred to a planting field. It will be another 12–15 months before it is harvested for the first time. Overall, the time from cutting to harvest is 2–3 years. Plants grown from cuttings have a life span of 30–40 years, while those grown from seeds can produce leaves for several hundred years. There are wild trees in China's Yunnan province estimated to be 2,000 years old.

2–3 years to grow
to maturity

After 5–7 years, the plant
is ready for plucking

PLUCKED BUD AND LEAVES

Hand-picked leaves should conform to industry standards: stems with 2–3 small leaves and tender buds are preferred for manufacture. This is considered a fine pluck.

PRUNING

The mature plant stands at 1–1.2m (3–4ft) high, and the goal is to have around 30 branches on a plant to maintain a good shape and height for plucking. Plants receive their first pruning after 2 years. This is done during the dormant season. Light pruning is done once a year thereafter, while heavy pruning, removing all the leaves and the secondary branches to encourage rejuvenation, takes place every 3–4 years.

TERROIR

As with wine, each tea has its own character, and even teas of the same variety differ in flavour from region to region. This is due to the variation in interdependent conditions, known as terroir, or the ecosystem, in which the tea plant is grown.

The specific conditions in which the tea plant is grown play a big part in influencing its development and quality. Natural factors, such as altitude, soil, and climatic conditions, influence the flavour and character of the leaves, as well as the amount of vitamins, minerals, and other compounds contained within them. While tea growers may hope for enough constants in the local environment to influence and control their harvest each year, nothing in nature is predetermined. Extreme weather, low rainfall, and poor soil may affect growth and, ultimately, the choices made for processing the leaves.

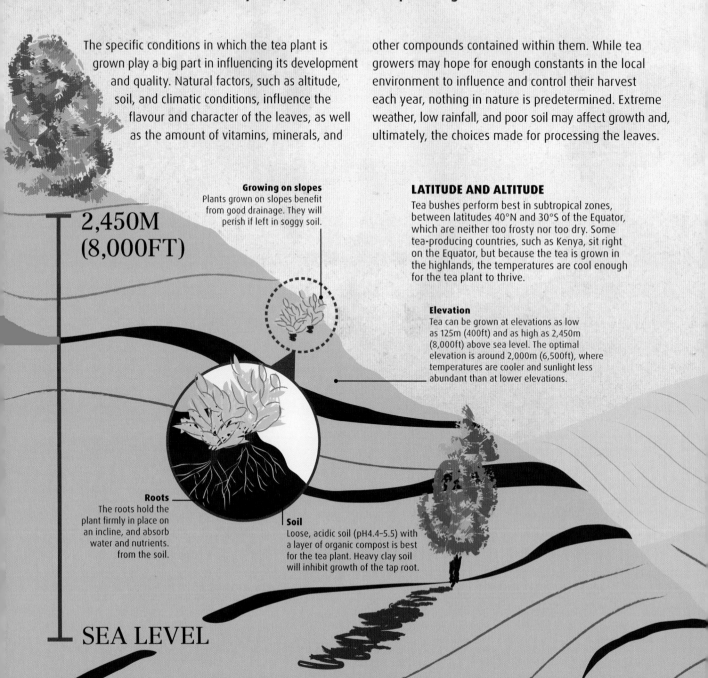

Growing on slopes
Plants grown on slopes benefit from good drainage. They will perish if left in soggy soil.

2,450M (8,000FT)

LATITUDE AND ALTITUDE

Tea bushes perform best in subtropical zones, between latitudes 40°N and 30°S of the Equator, which are neither too frosty nor too dry. Some tea-producing countries, such as Kenya, sit right on the Equator, but because the tea is grown in the highlands, the temperatures are cool enough for the tea plant to thrive.

Elevation
Tea can be grown at elevations as low as 125m (400ft) and as high as 2,450m (8,000ft) above sea level. The optimal elevation is around 2,000m (6,500ft), where temperatures are cooler and sunlight less abundant than at lower elevations.

Roots
The roots hold the plant firmly in place on an incline, and absorb water and nutrients from the soil.

Soil
Loose, acidic soil (pH4.4–5.5) with a layer of organic compost is best for the tea plant. Heavy clay soil will inhibit growth of the tap root.

SEA LEVEL

CLIMATE

The amount of rain, wind speeds and direction, and fluctuation in temperatures are crucial elements that can be the deciding factors for the success of a harvest.

Sun exposure
Tea plantations thrive when they can bask in 5 or more hours of sunlight per day.

Rain
Tea plants need a minimum of 1,500mm (60in) rainfall per year. Too much rainfall is harmful as the tea bush requires a dry period of 3–4 months per year to refresh its inner systems before the growing cycle begins again.

Clouds
Cloud cover regulates exposure to sunlight.

Slope orientation
When tea is grown on a slope, the incline's direction determines the hours of sunlight received.

Mist
Tea plants benefit from being shrouded in mist, as it provides moisture as well as protection from the sun.

Trees
Deciduous trees are often strategically planted throughout a tea garden to provide shade.

A TEA PLANTATION
A plantation in Kurseong, Darjeeling, India where carefully placed tall deciduous trees provide shade for the tea plants.

Shadows
The shadows cast by the trees help to regulate the temperature of the tea plants.

THE PRODUCTION PROCESS

The journey of tea from leaf to cup begins at the tea estate, where growers carefully nurture the leaf and prepare it for commercial production.

TYPES OF TEA ESTATES

Tea is grown on farms, or "estates", that vary hugely in size, and range from small "gardens", which are under 10 hectares (25 acres), to "plantations" spread over thousands of acres employing a large number of workers. While the aim remains the same regardless of the size of the tea estate, the difference lies in the intensity and scope of production. All estates tailor their tea to suit the taste of the market they cater to, and this influences the way the tea is grown and produced. Larger estates sell their yield by the tonne, at auction and through brokers, transporting it to its destination by container ships, while smaller estates often sell directly to importers, wholesalers, and retailers.

GARDENSCAPES
Some gardens form stunning undulating landscapes, while others are in straight rows.

INDUSTRIAL TEA ESTATES

As these estates grow tea mainly for commercial purposes, the focus is on quick and cheap production with few deviations from the tried and tested cultivars. Hence, large industrial tea estates use chemical fertilizers and pesticides to ensure a good harvest, and factory machinery to hasten the processing.

SINGLE ORIGIN ESTATES

Some large tea gardens take immense pride in their heritage. They are known for producing fine loose-leaf teas that are not blended with leaves from other farms. Known as single estate teas or single origin teas, these teas are valued for their unique flavour characteristics, which are particular to the terroir of the estate on which they are grown. As such, they don't strive to be consistent in flavour year on year in the same way as industrial tea estates.

ARTISAN GARDENS

Another category of tea estate is the artisan garden, which is smaller than a single origin estate, usually less than 10 hectares (25 acres). The success of an artisan garden lies in the grower's understanding of the tea plant's natural responses to its habitat, and their expertise in manipulating its plucked leaves. From tending the plant to sharing a cup with a buyer, the artisan tea maker has a hands-on approach throughout the entire process.

SINGLE ORIGIN

ONE OF A KIND
Teas from single origin estates are sought after for their signature style.

METHODS OF TEA PRODUCTION

When you make a cup of tea you will notice that some leaves resemble little grains of soil, while others look like they were just plucked from the tea plant. This difference is largely determined by the method of production used on the leaf. There are two methods for producing tea in a factory: the CTC (crush, tear, curl) method and the orthodox method.

Whole leaves are fed into the hopper.

The leaves are crushed, torn, and curled by large blades inside the machine.

The processed leaves come out of the other end, ready for oxidation.

CTC METHOD

Invented in the 1930s, this method involves the use of industrial machinery to process tea leaves. Large, thick leaves of a lower grade are blade-sliced, crushed, and bruised (to speed up oxidation), then machine-rolled into tiny grains of equal size before they undergo oxidation. This method is used exclusively in the production of black tea, and mostly for commodity tea (grown in industrial gardens for commercial uses). The CTC method is particularly prevalent in Sri Lanka, Kenya, and parts of India, but not in China.

ROTORVANE MACHINE
CTC factories use specialized machines, such as the rotorvane, to process the leaves.

ORTHODOX METHOD

Orthodox-style tea is wholly or partially handmade, and aims to preserve as much of the whole leaf as possible. It is the standard method of production for all teas, except commerical black tea, which is usually produced using the CTC method. The whole leaf is regarded as superior in quality; leaves that break are ranked using the British grading system (see p90) in India, Sri Lanka, and Kenya, and priced accordingly. More tea producers are adopting this method due to the increasing demand for this type of tea.

There is an inverse relationship between quality and quantity, and therefore price. Although the quantity produced may be lower, higher prices per gram make up the difference.

UNBROKEN LEAF
Whole, unbroken leaves are the aim of orthodox tea production. Dry leaves are fragile and may break during the last stages.

GRANULAR TEA
CTC tea is almost always destined for the tea bag because it's broken into very small dust-like pieces, known as fannings, that release their flavour very quickly.

PLANTATION TO TEAPOT

Producing tea is much more than just plucking leaves and drying them. The process involves a series of steps, each of them equally important, which take the leaves from the first plucking stage to the finished product.

Every country and region has a distinct way of producing tea. Handmade teas vary the most, from village to village and from maker to maker. However, there are universally accepted production processes that have been used for centuries. During the height of tea production in China, India, Japan, and Korea, tea producers work around the clock. There is a very short window for plucking, and once separated from the plant, the leaf starts to degrade.

TEA PRODUCTION PROCESS

Not all tea types go through the same stages of production. Some have lots of steps, such as black and oolong teas, while others, such as yellow tea, have minimal production. Use the key opposite to find a particular tea type and follow left to right, starting with plucking and moving through the various steps to completion.

PLUCKING

A tea plant is plucked over several growing periods – in early spring (notably in Darjeeling), when the first flush of young buds appear, again in early summer and, in some areas, in autumn. In equatorial regions, such as Kenya, tea is plucked year-round. On sloping terrain, tea is still hand-plucked – a laborious task performed mostly by women.

WITHERING

Fresh tea leaves contain 75 per cent moisture, which must be removed from the leaves to make them pliable for further processing. Leaves are spread out, either in the sun (white tea, Pu'er), or on trays in a controlled, well-ventilated factory environment where the temperature is kept at 20-24°C (68–75°F). The average wither is 20 hours, but varies from tea to tea.

ROLLING

Now that some of the moisture has left the leaf, the tea juices are more condensed and the leaf is ready to be shaped into rolled, twisted, or curled leaves. This stage breaks down the cell walls in the leaf and sets the leaf up for optimum oxidation for oolong and black teas, and brings the aromatics to the surface for green and yellow teas.

FIXING

This stage applies only to green and yellow tea, which do not go through an intentional factory withering, rather a short air drying to remove moisture. The leaves are "fixed" quickly under high heat to destroy enzymes and prevent oxidation. Fixing, also known as "kill green", is done by pan-firing. This preserves the aromas and volatile oils in the leaves.

FIRST FLUSH
A tea plucker picking tender
new buds in early spring, when
nutrients "flush" into the tips of
the plant after a dormant winter.

FERMENTATION

After rolling, Pu'er tea is steamed and formed
into cakes ready for fermentation. There are two
types of Pu'er: sheng (raw) and shou (ripe). Sheng
Pu'er is left to ferment naturally, culturing
micro-organisms slowly over many years, while
shou Pu'er is fermented, or aged, over several
months in humidity-controlled storage facilities.

OXIDATION

During oxidation, enzymes in the
leaf are transformed into theaflavins
(informing taste) and thearubigins
(informing colour). This is achieved
by spreading the leaves on tables
in a humid environment. The
process takes several hours, lasting
until the tea master decides that
oxidation has concluded (for black
tea), or that the desired level has
been reached (for oolong).

FIRING/DRYING

Originally done in a basket or
wok over charcoal, most tea
leaves are now dried in tumble
dryers. Some teas, such as
Lapsang Souchong black tea and
Long jing (Dragon Well) green tea,
still use a traditional method as a
signature of their style and flavour.
The finished leaf contains only 3
per cent moisture.

SORTING

Once processed, leaves are either
hand-sorted or machine-sorted.
Some machines have infrared
cameras that can detect various
sizes of leaf in order to sort them
into grades and separate out
unwanted elements, such as
stems. A well-produced, orthodox
tea will have fewer small pieces of
leaf and more whole leaves, which
are considered a higher grade.

HEAPING

After fixing, yellow tea goes through a step known as
"heaping", or "men huang". The leaves are laid out in piles
for a prolonged resting wrapped in damp cloth. The mixture
of heat and humidity gives the leaves a yellow cast.

ONE PLANT, MANY TEAS

Many types of tea are produced worldwide, all of which come from the same plant species. Each tea is produced differently and has unique features that affect flavour and strength. Here, they are grouped under the six main types. From sweet and fragrant to chocolatey and nutty, there is a spectrum of flavours to enjoy.

GREEN TEA

Green tea is unoxidized and most closely resembles the original plucked leaf – a small springtime leaf bud that contains abundant nutrients and oils sent up from the roots after a period of winter dormancy. Green tea is admired for its freshness and fleeting nature (it has a short shelf life of 6–8 months). The most prized green teas in China are referred to as pre-Qing Ming, or "before the spring festival", which falls in early April. Green tea comes in different shapes – flat, needle-like, curled like a snail, rolled into balls, or in fine twists.

Gyokuro
Japan

Anji Bai Cha
Zhejiang province, China

Long Jing
Zhejiang province, China

Zhu Ye Qing
Sichuan province, China

Matcha
Japan

Sencha
Japan

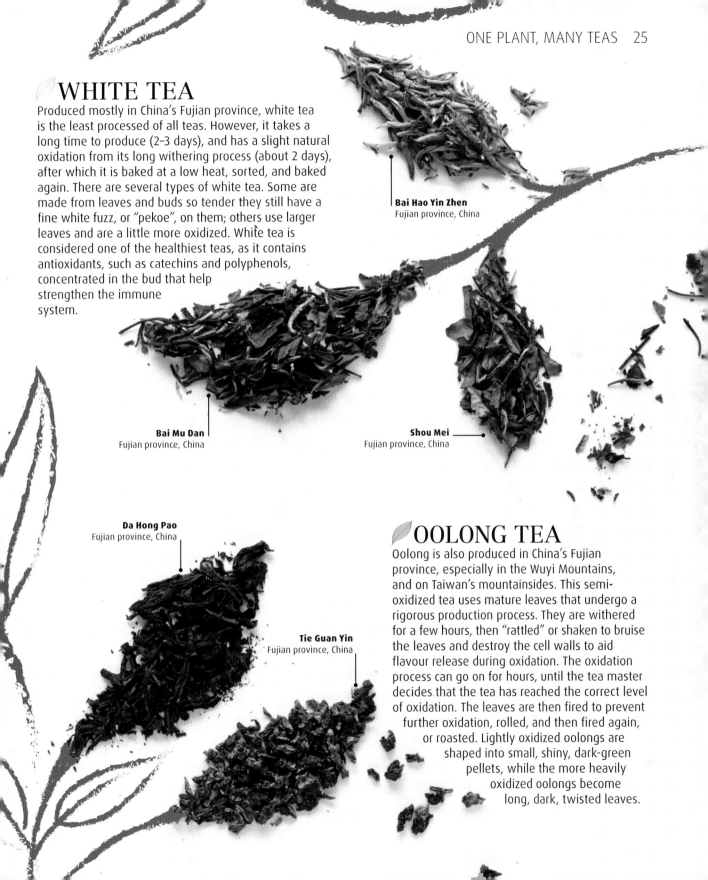

WHITE TEA

Produced mostly in China's Fujian province, white tea is the least processed of all teas. However, it takes a long time to produce (2–3 days), and has a slight natural oxidation from its long withering process (about 2 days), after which it is baked at a low heat, sorted, and baked again. There are several types of white tea. Some are made from leaves and buds so tender they still have a fine white fuzz, or "pekoe", on them; others use larger leaves and are a little more oxidized. White tea is considered one of the healthiest teas, as it contains antioxidants, such as catechins and polyphenols, concentrated in the bud that help strengthen the immune system.

Bai Hao Yin Zhen
Fujian province, China

Bai Mu Dan
Fujian province, China

Shou Mei
Fujian province, China

Da Hong Pao
Fujian province, China

Tie Guan Yin
Fujian province, China

OOLONG TEA

Oolong is also produced in China's Fujian province, especially in the Wuyi Mountains, and on Taiwan's mountainsides. This semi-oxidized tea uses mature leaves that undergo a rigorous production process. They are withered for a few hours, then "rattled" or shaken to bruise the leaves and destroy the cell walls to aid flavour release during oxidation. The oxidation process can go on for hours, until the tea master decides that the tea has reached the correct level of oxidation. The leaves are then fired to prevent further oxidation, rolled, and then fired again, or roasted. Lightly oxidized oolongs are shaped into small, shiny, dark-green pellets, while the more heavily oxidized oolongs become long, dark, twisted leaves.

BLACK TEA

A fully oxidized tea, black tea is produced in Kenya and many Asian countries, including Sri Lanka, China, and India. Much of the world's black tea is grown for the tea bag industry, and it is often mixed with other types of tea to make blends, such as breakfast and afternoon, which are enhanced by the addition of milk and/or sugar. The Chinese refer to black teas as "red teas" because of the colour of the liquid. Black teas are brisk, malty, full-bodied, and bracing because of the rich flavours that develop during the oxidation process.

Ceylon
Sri Lanka

Assam
Assam, India

**Darjeeling
First Flush**
West Bengal, India

**Darjeeling
Second Flush**
West Bengal, India

PU'ER TEA

Often referred to as a post-fermented tea, Pu'er is named after the town in which it is produced in China's Yunnan province. The tea contains micro-organisms with probiotic properties, which aid digestion and promote a healthy immune system, so is commonly consumed to aid weight loss. After the leaves are processed, they are steamed and pressed into cakes and aged for several years before they are sold; the tea is also available as loose leaves.

There are two kinds of Pu'er: Sheng (raw), which is allowed to develop and age naturally, and Shou (ripe), which undergoes an accelerated fermentation process. Similar teas are produced in other provinces of China and are referred to as "dark tea" or "hei cha". Post-fermented aged tea, particularly Pu'er, is highly sought-after by connoisseurs who store and age it for decades, as the flavours (which vary from earthy, musty, and leathery, to chocolatey or woody) become more complex over time.

Liu An Dark Tea
Anhui province, China

Sheng Pu'er Tuo Cha cake
Yunnan province, China

YELLOW TEA

Yellow tea is produced in only a few areas of China, such as the Hunan and Sichuan provinces. As a result, very little is produced or exported, making it fairly rare. As in the case of green tea, the best grades of yellow tea are produced from tea leaves harvested early in spring. Yellow tea is characterized by its fresh and delicate flavour, and gets its name from the leaf's slightly yellow cast, which is caused by the yellowing process it undergoes (see p23).

Jun Shan Yin Zhen
Dong Ting Lake,
Hunan province, China

**Mo Gan
Huang Ya**
Zhejiang province,
China

Meng Ding Huang Ya
Sichuan province, China

MATCHA

Brilliantly coloured and packed with antioxidants, Matcha is growing in popularity worldwide. This green tea, which has been around for over 1,000 years, is being touted as the "espresso of the tea world" for its strong, bold flavours and ability to perk you up.

THE WONDER DRINK

Matcha powder is a throwback to the Tang dynasty of China, when powdered tea was the norm. It was introduced to Japan by Buddhist monks who visited China and brought it back with them. It eventually became an integral part of the Japanese tea culture, being used in the Chanoyu tea ceremony. The best quality tea plants, destined to become Matcha, are grown in the Uji region of Japan.

Matcha's distinctive electric green colour is a result of artificial shading for several weeks just before harvest, which stimulates the production of chlorophyll. The leaf buds are then plucked, steamed, and dried, and the stems and veins are removed. These leaves, known as "tencha", are then placed in a Matcha grinder and milled to a fine powder between the grinder's two granite plates. It can take up to one hour to grind 30g (1oz) of Matcha.

Matcha has high caffeine levels and is packed with greater health-giving properties than regular green teas, as the whole leaf is consumed. It contains a number of antioxidants, including EGCg, which is known for its cancer-fighting properties, and L-theanine, which helps to calm the mind and improve memory and concentration.

There are two ceremonial grades of Matcha available: Usucha (thin) and Koicha (thick), as well as a lower grade, known as confectioner's grade. Usucha is the most widely available grade and is best used for everyday consumption. Koicha is mostly reserved for use in the formal Chanoyu ceremony. Confectioner's grade Matcha is the lowest quality grade and is much cheaper to buy, making it ideal for culinary use in macarons, cake, and ice cream.

Scoop

Chawan

MATCHA'S GREEN GOODNESS

As the whole leaf is consumed, the nutritional benefits of Matcha are far higher than that of other teas. Matcha helps to detox the body, improves the immune system, and boosts energy and metabolism.

IN MEDIEVAL JAPAN, SAMURAI WARRIORS DRANK MATCHA TO PREPARE FOR BATTLE

MATCHA LATTÉ
Creamy and frothy, the latté is a popular way to consume Matcha, as the milk (either dairy or plant) softens and smooths the flavour. See the delicious recipe for White Chocolate Matcha Latté on page 157.

Matcha powder

Chasen

MATCHA MACARONS
Matcha-infused macarons make a sweet snack with a hint of herbaceous goodness.

HOW TO PREPARE

Whisk up this rich and foamy tea for a quick hit of energy.

YOU WILL NEED

Ingredients

½–1 tsp Usucha grade Matcha powder

120–175ml (4–6fl oz) water heated to 75°C (170°F)

1 Place the Matcha powder in a chawan, or cereal bowl, and add a small amount of the hot water. Whisk the mixture to make a thick paste.

2 Add the remaining water to the mixture and whisk briskly using a "W" or "N" stroke, until the tea is smooth and frothy.

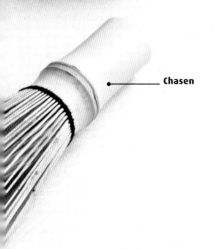

MATCHA CAKE
Add Matcha powder to the dry ingredients when making your cake or icing. Just 2–3 tablespoons will be enough to impart a bright green colour, but be careful not to add too much as the flavour may become bitter.

BLOOMING TEA

Blooming teas, or flower teas as they are also known, consist of fresh flowers encased in white tea leaves. When steeped, the bloom unfurls to reveal the flowers within.

Originating in the Fujian province of China, blooming teas are made by nimble-fingered women, who can make up to 400 blooms per day. With twists and turns of leaves, flowers, and thread, they produce compact balls of tea, about 2cm (³/₄in) in diameter.

White Silver Needle buds, which have been processed as green tea, are used for this process, as the young leaves are pliable, easy to work with, and look good while infusing. First, the leaves are carefully tied together at the base. Then, dried flowers, such as osmanthus, jasmine, chrysanthemum, lily, or marigold, are threaded together and bound with the tea leaves. The order in which the flowers are arranged will determine the style of the bloom.

Some styles symbolize happiness, prosperity, or love, while others portray concepts, such as a flower blooming in spring. The blooms are then bound together at the top and wrapped in cloth to hold them until they are heated, at a very high temperature, to secure their shape.

When selecting blooming tea, look for leaves that are whole, and flower colours that are not too pale.

Blooming teas look best when they are prepared in a glass teapot, but you can also use a preheated tall tumbler or glass jug. Place the bloom in a teapot. Heat the water to 75–80°C (170–175°F) and pour slowly over the bloom, filling two-thirds of the teapot. After 1–2 minutes, the bloom will begin to open and reveal the flowers and colours within.

As the white buds have been processed in the same way as green tea, you can expect several infusions from each bloom. Once you have consumed the tea, you can continue to display the flower for several days in a jug of fresh, cold water.

AN EXPERIENCED CRAFTSPERSON CAN TIE MORE THAN 400 BLOOMS A DAY

HEALTH BENEFITS OF TEA

Tea is packed with antioxidants and chemicals, such as polyphenols, L-theanine, and catechins that help to fortify the immune system. Of all teas, green and white are the most beneficial as they are made from young leaves full of these chemicals, and are the least processed.

Tea was first used as a medicinal beverage in China to regulate internal body temperature and stimulate the mind. When it reached Europe in the 17th century, it was sold in apothecary shops as a tonic and digestive. It was only in the first part of the 18th century that it was embraced as a social beverage. Tea has since developed into an everyday drink valued for its health-improving properties.

Many scientists have studied the health-giving qualities of tea, but there is still a great deal to discover. While all teas produced from the *Camelia sinensis* plant are good for health, many studies have looked at the effects of green tea extracts in particular, and most recommend drinking at least three cups of tea per day to gain the health benefits.

TEA AND YOUR BODY

While drinking tea will contribute to overall health and well-being, it is becoming evident that the many unique compounds in tea target specific areas of the body, providing protection from stress and disease, and strengthening the bones and the immune system. From oral health to digestive health, tea is now valued as much for its beneficial attributes as for its delicious flavours.

DENTAL HEALTH
The antimicrobial qualities of tea help to prevent dental cavities and bad breath caused by bacteria, while the fluoride in tea strengthens the teeth. More mature leaves, such as those harvested for oolongs, contain higher levels of fluoride.

SKIN DEEP
The detoxifying effects of the antioxidants found in tea can help to regenerate and repair cells and protect the skin from harmful free radicals (damaged molecules). Despite the caffeine, tea is hydrating as it is mostly water.

IT'S ALL IN YOUR HEAD

Polyphenols, found in all types of tea, are believed to reduce the risk of degenerative diseases, as they protect the sections of the brain responsible for learning and memory.

STRESS TEST

Tea is a powerful stress buster. Green tea, in particular, contains a unique amino acid, *L-theanine*, which increases Alpha waves in the brain, relaxes the mind, and, combined with caffeine, promotes alertness.

CAFFEINE

Tea contains caffeine, a bitter compound that stimulates the nervous system. It is one of the various compounds sent from the roots of the plant to protect and nourish the buds as they grow, and is known to repel insect attack.

There are similar amounts of caffeine in tea, per dry leaf weight, to coffee. However, the polyphenols (tannins) in tea regulate and slow the release of caffeine, so that the feeling of alertness it gives lasts much longer. Caffeine levels in tea depend on the type of tea used, the water temperature, the steeping time, and the time of year the tea leaves are picked.

GREEN AND WHITE TEAS CONTAIN HIGHER LEVELS OF ANTIOXIDANTS THAN BLACK AND OOLONG

HEART TO HEART

The polyphenols in tea are a rich source of flavonoid antioxidants and neutralize the toxic and mutating effects of free radicals, helping to prevent cancer. Flavonoids, found in tea, help protect the heart from cardiovascular disease. Drinking green tea may also significantly reduce the risk of high blood pressure.

EASY TO STOMACH

Tea, oolong in particular, has long been used as a post-meal digestive drink. Pu'er is particularly good for digestion because of its probiotic properties, and has been touted as a fat-burning tool. Green tea can help to stimulate metabolism and burn calories.

FEEL IT IN YOUR BONES

Tea drinkers are believed to have higher bone density than non-tea drinkers due to the high levels of fluoride in tea.

THE PERFECT INFUSION

LOOSE-LEAF OR TEA BAG TEA?

Since the invention of the tea bag, people have debated its merits over loose-leaf tea. While it is hard to contest the convenience of tea bags, when it comes to flavour, the scales tip sharply in favour of loose-leaf tea.

LOOSE LEAF

Preparing loose-leaf tea may require a little more effort than a tea bag, but it is still very simple, and makes a world of difference to the quality of your cuppa.

CONVENIENCE

Special equipment, such as the mesh infuser, makes preparing and cleaning up loose-leaf tea quick and easy.

FRESHNESS AND QUALITY

Whole leaves have less exposed surface area than tea bag "fannings" or CTC leaf (see opposite), so will stay fresher for longer, if stored correctly.

FLAVOUR

Loose leaf tea is made up of whole leaves, or large pieces of leaf, still containing aromatic oils, which make a complex, full-flavoured cup.

VALUE

A common misconception is that loose-leaf tea is expensive. Making a cup of tea requires only small amounts of loose leaf. It is also possible to have multiple infusions of some teas, such as oolong, lowering the price per cup.

ENVIRONMENTAL FRIENDLINESS

Loose leaves are biodegradable, and break down in the soil quickly, so are good for composting.

INFUSION

Loose leaves release their flavour slowly into the water. This means their strength isn't spent all at once, saving some character for further infusions.

You will be able to pick out certain flavours of the tea from its aroma.

Tea leaves release more aroma and flavour when they have ample space to infuse.

The infuser contains the leaves and makes cleaning easier.

TEA BAG

The tea bag was an accidental invention. In 1908, Thomas Sullivan, a tea merchant from New York City, sent his clients samples of tea in small silk drawstring bags. He expected them to remove the leaves from the bag before infusing them, but they brewed the tea directly, in the bags, and were so pleased with the results that they asked for more to be sent similarly packaged.

Tea bags are available in round or square sachets (above), which leave little room for the leaves to infuse. The pyramid tea bag (left) is shaped to enable better infusion as the water infiltrates it.

The pyramid tea bag has more infusing space than square or round tea bags.

TEA BAG FANNINGS

Commercial black tea bags contain "fannings", or pieces of tea leaves considered unsuitable to be sold loose.

CONVENIENCE

The tea bag is convenient to use as it comes in pre-measured packs, and eliminates the need for a strainer, teapot, or infuser.

FRESHNESS AND QUALITY

Commercial tea bags are filled with the smallest pieces of the lowest grade commodity black tea. This is one of the reasons why they infuse so quickly, but also why they become stale, regardless of how they are stored, as their surface area is exposed.

FLAVOUR

The tea used in tea bags loses many of its essential oils and much of its aroma during processing. As such, tea bags have less complexity of flavour than loose-leaf tea. They also release more tannins when infused, which can result in a bitter and astringent drink.

VALUE

A large box of tea bags is relatively inexpensive, but the price per cup is similar to that of loose leaf, especially when you consider that loose-leaf tea can be used for multiple infusions and tea bags only once. Tea bags also have a shorter shelf life.

ENVIRONMENTAL FRIENDLINESS

Although some types of tea bag are fully biodegradable, the majority contain small amounts of plastic (polypropylene) that will remain in a compost pile for years. Look for bags that are polypropylene-free.

INFUSION

Tea bags are easy to infuse, even without a teapot, but restrict the movement of tea leaves that is required to make a really good cup of tea.

HOW TO STORE TEA

Loose-leaf tea should be stored properly as it is vulnerable to light, air, and moisture. Tea's sponge-like dry leaves soak up any flavours and aromas they come into contact with, so keep them airtight, cool, and dry.

SHELF LIFE

Even though the tea leaf feels very dry, it contains 3 per cent moisture and volatile oils, which are vital to its flavour. These oils will evaporate if the leaves are not stored properly. Green tea has the shortest shelf life at 6–8 months, while oolong lasts 1–2 years. Black tea has the longest shelf life of over 2 years, but if it is flavoured or has added spices or fruits, it may degrade more quickly. Follow these guidelines to ensure that your tea stays fresh a little longer.

BUY IN SMALL QUANTITIES
Large amounts of tea will probably be sitting in the cupboard for a long time. Take advantage of sample sizes or "taster packs" as this is the best way to try a new tea without having to dedicate space and storage containers for something you may not like.

BUY THIS YEAR'S HARVEST
Always start with fresh tea. If the purchase is this year's harvest, it has a better chance of lasting the full shelf life.

KEEP IT COOL
Store in a cool, dry area, ideally a low cupboard, but not in the fridge. It is important to store the leaves away from spices and any source of heat.

SEAL IT UP
If storing the leaves in a bag, make sure it can be tightly sealed after each use.

DO

KEEP IT AIRTIGHT
Store in an opaque tea caddy made of tin, ceramics, or stainless steel. Making sure the container is airtight will prevent any odours from permeating the leaves.

CHOOSE FANCY STORAGE
Celebrate your tea by storing it in a special container or tea caddy. If using an antique, check the lining to make sure it is not made of lead.

IF STORED PROPERLY, BLACK TEA WILL KEEP WELL FOR TWO YEARS OR MORE

EXPOSE TO LIGHT
Avoid storing in a see-through container, as light will degrade the leaves more quickly and lighten their colour.

GO OVERBOARD
Curb your enthusiasm to try every new tea. Your cupboard will be brimming over with tea that you may not get around to trying for several years.

STORE ABOVE THE OVEN OR HOB
The heat rising from the oven will weaken the flavours of the tea.

STORE IN THE FRIDGE
The tea leaves will absorb moisture through the process of condensation.

STORE WITH OTHER TEAS
Different styles or flavours should not be stored together in one container as they will leach into one another.

STORE IN UNLINED WOODEN CONTAINERS
Always line a wooden container before storing, unless the tea is first put in an air-tight plastic bag. Loose-fitting lids will allow moisture into the tea causing it to become stale or even mouldy.

KEEP WITH SPICES
Storing tea with spices could spell disaster for your tea. Tea leaves are porous and will suck in the other aromas floating around the cupboard.

BUY OLD TEA
Always find out how old the tea is when you buy it, and use it according to its shelf life.

DON'T

CUPPING LIKE A PROFESSIONAL

Professional tea tasters practise tea tasting, known as "cupping", to evaluate the specific qualities of a tea. By training your sense of smell and taste, you will begin to identify and appreciate the complex flavours of different teas.

PROFESSIONAL TEA TASTERS

Considered masters of their craft, professional tea tasters and blenders "cup" hundreds of teas every day. Having developed their senses of smell and taste over years of experience, they know which characteristics to look for and which to reject. This process of evaluating tea to determine the best features and imperfections of the leaves is called "cupping". Standard procedures are used for every cup: 1 tsp of leaves is infused in 125ml (4½fl oz) boiling water for 5 minutes, no matter what the type of tea. While non-professionals may find it unpleasantly bitter, this helps the tasters to select leaves that will best match the profile of their tea blend and determine a new "formula" of blends for each harvest. Their goal is to achieve consistency in a blend from an inconsistent tea harvest.

TASTING SET

A professional tasting set consists of a tasting bowl and a small lidded cup with a handle and groove on the rim to strain out the leaves. Dry leaves are placed in the cup, and boiling water is poured over. The lid is placed on the cup, and the tea is allowed to steep for 5 minutes. Then the cup, with the lid still on, is tipped sideways into the tasting bowl to let the tea flow into it. The used leaves are removed from the cup and placed on the inverted lid.

ALL FIVE SENSES ARE INVOLVED THROUGHOUT EVERY STAGE OF TASTING

TASTING AT HOME

Professional tasting is not done for enjoyment, but you can have fun exploring the flavours and characteristics of different teas in your own home. With an open mind, a tasting can allow you to discover new teas.

YOU WILL NEED

1 tsp tea leaves per person, such as green, oolong, and black, or a "flight" of 3 types of tea, for example, Darjeeling

tea pot, or tea cup with a lid or small saucer to cover

almonds or pumpkin seeds, to neutralize your palate between tastings

Do not wear fragrance when tasting tea, as it will interfere with your sense of smell when trying to isolate aromas.

1 Examine the dry leaf and note its colour, shape, size, and fragrance. Place 1 tsp tea leaves for each person into your tea pot or cup. Add 175ml (6fl oz) water per tsp tea leaf, at the appropriate temperature, cover with the lid or small saucer, and leave to steep. Refer to pages 42–47 for guidance on the infusion time for each type of tea.

2 Remove the lid and put your ear to the leaves. Notice the slight popping sound of the leaves unfurling.

3 The aroma should begin to waft as the water touches the leaves. To get a sense of how the tea will taste, lift the lid and hold it to your nose once the infusion is ready. Volatile oils will have started to evaporate from the infusion.

4 Strain the tea into tasting cups. Then examine the wet leaves carefully, and take in the aroma.

5 Notice the colour of the tea. Inhale, then take a quick slurp to draw the flavours to all the taste receptors around the tongue. Notice how the tea feels; this is the "mouthfeel" of the tea. Some key flavours are shown on the flavour wheel (see pp50–51) to help you describe the tea.

GETTING THE MOST FROM YOUR TEA

Each type of tea has a distinct character, and displays a flavour, colour, and aroma that is decidedly its own. The following guidelines will help you experience the full flavour potential of the teas, but as enjoyment is paramount, feel free to adapt the guidelines to your taste.

GREEN TEA

At its best, green tea will bring a freshness reminiscent of open meadows or sea air. Start with a leaf less than one year old, and pay attention to water temperature: too much heat will kill the gentle amino acids that sweeten the tea, while water that is too cool will prevent the flavour from developing fully.

Steeping time is very important for green teas. As an oversteeped tea can be astringent and bitter, it is best to start with a short steep, taste it, and increase the steeping time by 30 seconds, until it suits your palate.

PREPARATION GUIDELINES

Tea shown here: Bi Luo Chun (Green Snail Springtime), from Dong Ting mountain, Jiangsu province, China

Measure: 1 tbsp for 175ml (6fl oz) water

Water temperature: 75°C (170°F) for Chinese teas; 65°C (150°F) for Japanese teas. Use spring water, if possible.

Infusion: Test with a short steep, and increase steeping time by 30 seconds for each infusion. Can be used for 3–4 infusions.

DRY LEAVES
Green tea leaves may be light or dark green, and come in many shapes and sizes, from thin, twisted, and dusty as in this example, to flat, shiny, and bud-like.

WET LEAVES
During infusion, the tea unravels to reveal buds and leaves.

LIQUOR
The infused and strained tea, also known as liquor, is pale green, with a hint of yellow. The brew is fresh and bright, with soft, fruity flavours.

WHITE TEA

Considered the most nuanced and subtle of teas, white tea contains a number of healthy compounds including polyphenols. It is an early tea, picked just as the first buds appear, and therefore given high status in the Chinese tea world. It can be a challenge to appreciate this subtler tea with layered flavours, especially for those who prefer rich black teas.

   There is only a handful of styles of white tea: Bai Hao Yin Zhen (Silver Needles) is the highest quality, and is divided into even more refined groups, with pricing reflecting the quality. Bai Mu Dan (White Peony), a more affordable style, contains silver buds as well as large leaves.

PREPARATION GUIDELINES

Tea shown here: Bai Mu Dan (White Peony), from Fuding, Fujian province, China

Measure: 2 tbsp for 175ml (6fl oz) water

Water temperature: 85°C (185°F). Use spring water, if possible.

Infusion: Steep for 2 minutes, and increase steep time by 30 seconds for each infusion. Can be used for 2–3 infusions.

DRY LEAVES
White tea leaves have silver buds with larger, brittle, dark green or brown leaves.

WET LEAVES
When infused, the tea displays velvety buds, large, green, multi-shaded leaves, and twigs.

LIQUOR
Light golden in colour, the infusion has a sweet aroma, with flavours of pine, sweetcorn, and burnt sugar.

OOLONG TEA

There is a wide range of oolongs available, each with different oxidation levels, aromas, and flavours. A green oolong, such as Ali Shan from Taiwan, may have a 35 per cent oxidation level and a floral aroma, while a Wuyi Rock could have an 80 per cent oxidation level and rich, roasted, earthy notes.

Oolongs are among the most difficult teas to produce, as their quality depends on the skill of their producer. Although this semi-oxidized tea literally takes a beating during processing, oolong is very forgiving, and can be used for multiple infusions, presenting new flavours each time.

PREPARATION GUIDELINES

Tea shown here: Ali Shan oolong, from Ali mountain, Nantou, Taiwan

Measure: 2 tsp for 175 ml (6fl oz) water.

Water temperature: 85°C (185°F) for lightly oxidized oolongs; 95°C (200°F) for heavily oxidized oolongs.

Infusion: Warm the steeping vessel first, and rinse the leaves with hot water before steeping for 1–2 minutes. Increase steeping time by 1 minute for each subsequent infusion. May be used for up to 10 infusions.

DRY LEAVES
The medium to dark jade green leaves of this lightly oxidized oolong are rolled into tight balls, some retaining their stems.

WET LEAVES
With each infusion, the leaves unfurl to reveal large, thick, shiny leaves with redness around the edges (indicating where the oxidation occurred).

LIQUOR
The bright yellow liquor is sweet and fragrant, and has slight citrus and floral notes. Each subsequent infusion reveals new flavours.

DRY LEAVES
Some Darjeeling dry leaves have a slight green colour, and may be whole or broken.

LIQUOR
This golden liquor of Darjeeling tastes of apple and spice, and has an aroma reminiscent of muscatel grapes.

WET LEAVES
While infused Darjeeling leaves appear brown and green, the wet leaves of other black teas may be mahogany, walnut, or even golden in colour.

BLACK TEA

Black tea is the most well-known tea in the western world. Familiarity with black tea usually begins with tea-bag tea and famous blends, such as English Breakfast. This familiarity might lead us to expect the same character from all black teas, but there are many varieties with complex flavours and characteristics.

Black tea is fully oxidized, its polyphenols having converted to thearubigins (colour) and theaflavonoids (flavour). Heftier varieties, such as Assam, can be complemented with milk and/or sugar, but it is better to taste a delicate tea, such as a first flush Darjeeling, in its natural state, before deciding to add anything.

Historically, most premium black tea is produced in India or Sri Lanka, but owing to its growing popularity among the Chinese, black tea production is set to increase in that region.

PREPARATION GUIDELINES

Tea shown here: First flush Darjeeling, from Darjeeling, India

Measure: 2 tsp for 175ml (6fl oz) water

Water Temperature: 100°C (210°F)

Infusion: Steep for 2 minutes. Some whole-leaf black teas, such as Darjeeing or Chinese black teas, may be infused a second time. For these, add 1–2 minutes to the infusion time.

PU'ER TEA

Pu'er, or dark tea, is the only tea that contains probiotics, or "good" microbes. It can be aged for many years, and increases in value accordingly.

This tea is most commonly available in cake or brick form, but is also available as loose leaves, sometimes aged in bamboo. If you're using pressed Pu'er, try not to break the leaves when prying them from the cake, as this will damage them, making the tea bitter. Look for production dates on the wrapper. Pu'er continues to ripen and age over time, so can be kept for many years and tasted each year to experience the developing flavours.

PREPARATION GUIDELINES

Tea shown here: Shou Pu'er cake, 2010, from Yongde County, Yunnan province, China

Measure: 1 tsp for 175ml (6fl oz) water

Water temperature: 95°C (200°F)

Infusion: Rinse with hot water first, to soften the leaves for steeping, then steep for 2 minutes. Increase steeping time for 1 minute for each infusion. Can be used for 3–4 infusions.

WET LEAVES
After steeping, the whole leaves may vary from green to brown to black.

LIQUOR
This rich, opaque dark brown or purple brew tastes of leather, and dark, dried cherries.

DRY LEAVES
Pu'er in cake form has long, medium to dark brown and, sometimes, green leaves pressed into shape.

DRY LEAVES
Yellow tea has small, light
green buds, with some
golden yellow touches,
and fine white pekoe.

LIQUOR
The yellow brew has an initial
vegetal flavour, followed by
a sweet finish.

WET LEAVES
When infused, the
leaves resemble
miniature mangetout,
with streaks of yellow.

YELLOW TEA

Rare, but well worth seeking out, yellow tea is
made from the youngest tea buds. It is grown only
in China and there are just a few types of yellow
tea available, such as Meng Ding Huang Ya (Meng
Ding Mountain Yellow Sprout) from Sichuan
province and Jun Shan Yin Zhen (Jun Mountain
Silver Needle) from Hunan province. Yellow
tea is rich in amino acids, polyphenols,
polysaccharides, and vitamins that are
beneficial for the spleen and stomach
and aid digestion and weight loss.

PREPARATION GUIDELINES

Tea shown here: Jun Shan Yin Zhen, from
Hunan province, China

Measure: 1½ tsp for 175ml (6fl oz) water

Water temperature: 80°C (175°F). Use spring
water, if possible.

Infusion: Steep for 1–2 minutes. Increase
the steeping time by a further minute for
each infusion. Can be infused 2–3 times.

THE SCIENCE OF FLAVOUR

To identify the flavour of the tea you are drinking, the brain calls on taste stimuli from receptors on the tongue, olfactory stimuli from the nasal passage, and the textural and thermal sensations you experience while drinking.

There are hundreds of different flavour compounds in tea, but the average person can categorize only a few. With some concentration and a little experience, it is possible to train your brain to identify them. Take a look at the flavour wheel on pages 50–51 to identify some of the key flavours in tea.

SENSES

When thinking about identifying flavours, it is important to understand how senses work with one another. The cup illustration, right, helps you to understand how texture and taste work together to form your experience of astringency in the cup. Likewise taste and smell do not exist in isolation, but rather meet within the olfactory system to give you the experience of flavour.

FLAVOUR
Flavour is the combination of smell and taste, and this is what we experience when eating or drinking. Taste is closely tied to smell – 75 per cent of what we taste is determined by smell. Volatile aromatic oils in tea evaporate and rise into our nasal passages as we sip, creating flavours that can only be detected when the senses of smell and taste work together.

SMELL
Even before you sip tea, you will notice its aroma. While it is hot, you will smell wafts of the tea's bouquet in the air near the surface of the liquid. As you bring your nose close to the surface of the tea and sniff, you will engage the olfactory system. After inhaling, exhale through your nose. Aromas linger in the nasal passage, preparing your senses for the experience of taste inside your mouth.

TEMPERATURE

Temperature plays an important role in the sensory perception of tea. When tea is hot, aromas evaporate more quickly and certain layers of flavour disappear from the cup as it cools. Studies have shown that the tongue detects more astringency in a hot drink than a cool one, so it would benefit your experience of tasting delicately flavoured teas, such as white tea, to let them cool slightly before attempting to identify flavours.

TASTE

The tongue's taste buds contain taste receptors that feed messages to the brain. When we sip tea, saliva is secreted and flavours are changed and moderated. To taste and evaluate the character of a tea, slurp rapidly to spread the tea over all the receptors on the tongue.

ASTRINGENCY

Taste and texture come together to create astringency, an important characteristic of tea. It is the puckering or drying sensation in the mouth caused by the chemical reaction of the tea with saliva. Astringency occurs in varying degrees, depending on the amount of polyphenols (tannins) released during the tea's infusion. Tea connoisseurs value astringency in the right amount, but too much is unpleasant.

TEXTURE

You will feel the texture of tea when it comes into contact with the teeth and the mucous membranes lining the inside of the mouth. This is often referred to as "mouthfeel". The astringency, body, and smoothness of the tea determine the texture. Teas with low astringency might have a "soft mouthfeel", while teas with a high degree of astringency might have a "fuzzy mouthfeel".

THE TONGUE

Covered with 10,000 taste buds, each containing 50–100 taste receptor cells, the tongue is capable of identifying five basic tastes: sweet, salty, sour, bitter, and umami (a Japanese term meaning "pleasant savoury taste"), each in a specific area.

The diagram below illustrates what is commonly known as the "tongue map". It shows each distinct area of the tongue with the receptors for sweet on the tip, receptors for salt on either side of the front of the tongue, sour receptors on either side behind this, and bitter receptors at the back. Umami is detected in the centre of the tongue, which scientists had previously thought to be taste blind. When tasting tea, it's important to make sure the liquor reaches each of the five taste areas of the tongue so you are able to experience all of the flavours.

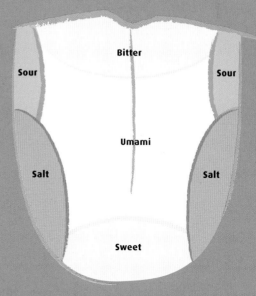

QUICKLY SLURP THE TEA TO STRIKE ALL OF THE TASTE RECEPTORS ON THE TONGUE

FLAVOUR APPRECIATION

When drinking tea, it may be difficult to distinguish between flavours. The "flavour wheel", a visual representation of the distinct flavours and aromas found in teas, is a handy guide that will help you to understand and appreciate the intricacies of flavour.

Evaluating tea using taste receptors in the mouth and nose opens us up to a world of broad flavour profiles, here categorized into 12 groups. Each group can then be further dissected into descriptors that allow you to analyse facets of the tea's flavours and characteristics.

Refer to the wheel after first smelling the aroma and then sipping the liquid infusion of the tea. Your first response will come from the inner wheel. For example: the green tea Bai Luo Chun (Green Snail Springtime) will immediately evoke vegetal, sweet, and nutty flavours.

Take another sip or sniff the wet leaves and look towards the smaller sections within this category. You may now detect the sweetness of corn in the vegetal category and the more specific flavour of chestnuts in the nutty section. Experimentation and experience will help you identify the flavours in any tea.

THE MORE YOU TASTE, THE EASIER IT IS TO IDENTIFY FLAVOURS

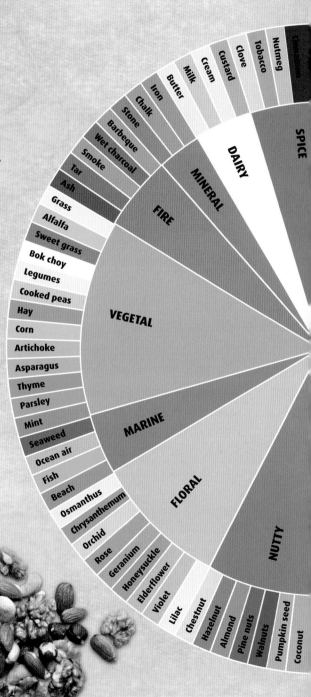

NUTS
Nuts define roasted and sweet flavours in all types of tea. They are good descriptors for the astringency of tea's tannins.

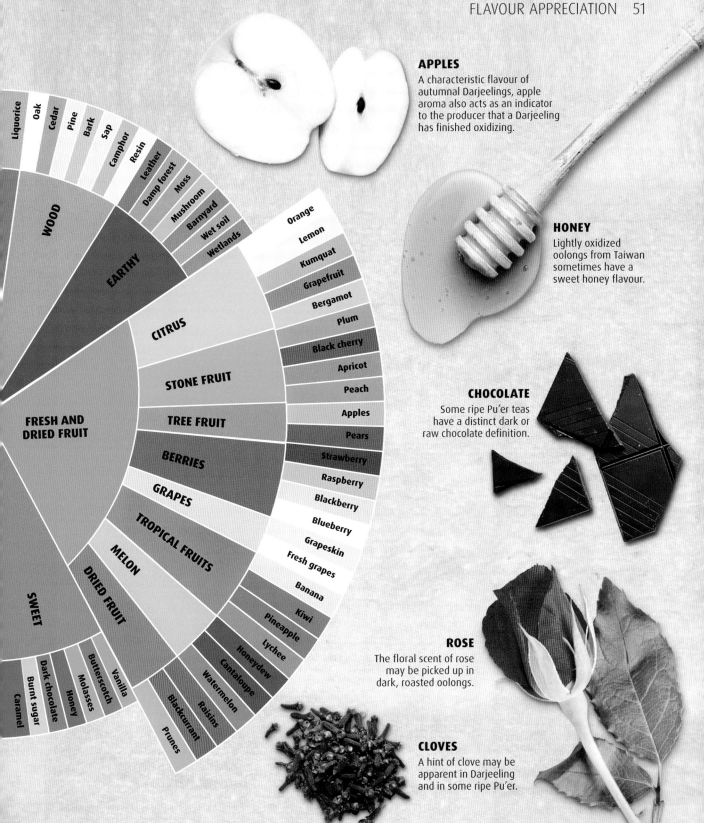

APPLES
A characteristic flavour of autumnal Darjeelings, apple aroma also acts as an indicator to the producer that a Darjeeling has finished oxidizing.

HONEY
Lightly oxidized oolongs from Taiwan sometimes have a sweet honey flavour.

CHOCOLATE
Some ripe Pu'er teas have a distinct dark or raw chocolate definition.

ROSE
The floral scent of rose may be picked up in dark, roasted oolongs.

CLOVES
A hint of clove may be apparent in Darjeeling and in some ripe Pu'er.

Flavour wheel labels:

WOOD — Liquorice, Oak, Cedar, Pine, Bark, Sap, Camphor, Resin

EARTHY — Leather, Damp forest, Moss, Mushroom, Barnyard, Wet soil, Wetlands

FRESH AND DRIED FRUIT

CITRUS — Orange, Lemon, Kumquat, Grapefruit, Bergamot

STONE FRUIT — Plum, Black cherry, Apricot, Peach

TREE FRUIT — Apples, Pears

BERRIES — Strawberry, Raspberry, Blackberry, Blueberry

GRAPES — Grapeskin, Fresh grapes

TROPICAL FRUITS — Banana, Kiwi, Pineapple, Lychee

MELON — Honeydew, Cantaloupe, Watermelon

DRIED FRUIT — Blackcurrant, Raisins, Prunes

SWEET — Caramel, Burnt sugar, Honey, Molasses, Butterscotch, Vanilla, Dark chocolate

WATER

According to an ancient Chinese proverb, water is the "mother of tea". As it makes up 99 per cent of a cup of tea, there is some truth to this. The quality of water you infuse with has a major impact on the flavour of your tea. To get the best out of your tea leaves, use clean and odourless water that has been heated to the right temperature.

Rainfall, pollution, and the local aquifer (porous underground rock from which groundwater is extracted) all affect your local water source, whether rural or urban. These factors influence the mineral and odour content of the water and its pH – the measurement, from 0–14, of acidity (at the low end) or alkalinity (at the high end) in liquids.

Generally, water has a neutral pH of 7, but sometimes tap water can be a little too alkaline or acidic for tea. Tap water also contains dissolved gases, which might have odours, or could be highly mineralized, which can overpower the delicate flavours in the infusion.

If you don't have a filter attached to your water system that dispenses pure water for tea, you can try using these alternatives:

Bottled spring water Not to be confused with mineral water, which is unsuitable due to the minerals added; look for spring water with 50–100ppm dissolved mineral salt content. Higher amounts will give a heavy mineral flavour to the tea.

Filtered tap water Portable water filter jugs work well to filter out unwanted odours and minerals from tap water. Change the filter as recommended.

Distilled water mixed with tap water Distilled water is flat and unappealing, but adding it to tap water that has a high mineral content will make it suitable for tea. Experiment with various ratios depending on the quality of your tap water.

WATER TEMPERATURES

Boiling point varies according to elevation. If you live in an area over 1,300m (4,265ft) above sea level, your water will not have reached 100°C (210°F) when your kettle clicks off. To compensate for this, add an extra half teaspoon of tea leaves per person and leave the infusion for a few extra minutes.

THE RIGHT HEAT
If the water for the infusion is too hot, the tea will be bitter and lose its aroma; if too cold, the tea will not infuse properly.

FINDING THE RIGHT TEMPERATURE

Heating the water to the correct temperature is key to making a good cup of tea. A fresh, fragile green leaf will be scalded if boiling water is poured over; partially oxidized teas, such as oolongs, will need hotter, but not boiling, water, and fully oxidized black teas will need boiling water to release their flavours. Whatever the desired infusion temperature, always begin with freshly drawn cool water.

If you don't have a variable temperature kettle, boil the water and let it sit in the kettle with the lid open for 5 minutes for green, white, and yellow teas; 3 minutes for oolong; and 2 minutes for Pu'er and other dark teas.

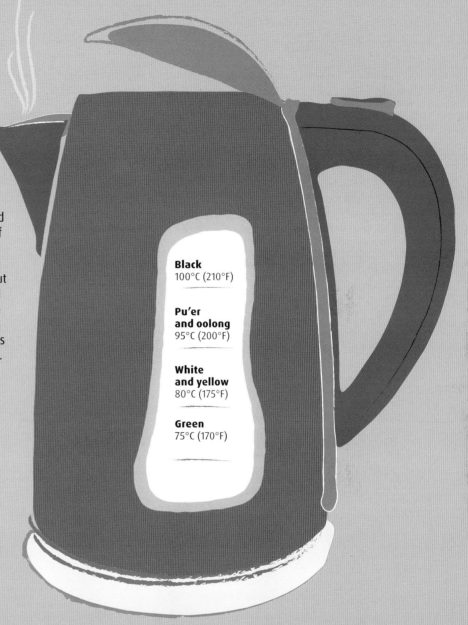

Black
100°C (210°F)

Pu'er and oolong
95°C (200°F)

White and yellow
80°C (175°F)

Green
75°C (170°F)

THE OPTIMUM WATER FOR TEA HAS A NEUTRAL PH OF 7, LOW DISSOLVED MINERAL CONTENT, AND NO CHLORINE OR OTHER GASEOUS ODOURS

TEA-MAKING EQUIPMENT

Tea shops offer a baffling array of teaware designed for a superlative tea experience. Assuming that the tea will be prepared using loose leaves, and that they need room to expand, here are some of the best choices that are available.

PORCELAIN TEAPOTS WITH INFUSERS

The classic teapot comes in a variety of sizes. A 3-cup pot (750ml/1¼ pints) will serve two people with a little extra for refills. Pouring the hot water into the pot from a height of about 25cm (10in) will "push" the leaves a bit and speed up the flavour release. To avoid a bitter liquor, always remove the infuser once the tea is ready.

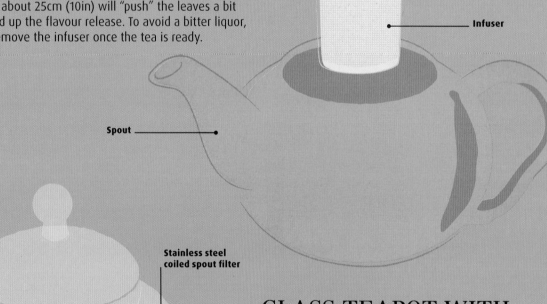

Lid

Infuser

Spout

Stainless steel coiled spout filter

GLASS TEAPOT WITH COILED SPOUT FILTER

A glass teapot has all the conveniences of other infuser teapots and the added benefit of enabling you to watch the leaves swirl through the water, releasing their colours. The stainless steel coiled spout filter stops the leaves escaping from the teapot as the liquid is poured into the cup.

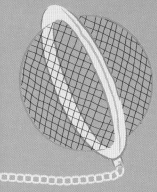

TEA BALL INFUSERS

These come in many forms, ranging from the classic ball, to a host of novelty shapes. Most hook onto the sides of mugs or teapots. All do the job well, but some inhibit the leaves from expanding, so make sure there is enough room in the infuser, and do not fill it to the brim with dry leaves.

Mesh

Lid

MUGS WITH STAINLESS STEEL MESH INFUSERS

Mug infusers are relatively easy to clean after use, so they are ideal for infusing tea without too much fuss. They function quite well, giving the leaves lots of room to deliver their flavour. Those with lids offer the best infusion because they preserve the aromas released by the leaves.

Panel with preset temperatures

VARIABLE TEMPERATURE KETTLES

These easy-to-use kettles have accurate temperature settings for each type of tea; simply select the tea type and press the button. Others have temperature settings, so it is necessary to know the optimal temperature for each type of tea (see pp42–47). Some models even allow you to infuse the leaves in the kettle.

GAIWAN

Used in China to prepare tea, the "gaiwan", or "lidded bowl", comes with a saucer and holds about 175ml (6fl oz) of liquid, the same size as a classic china teacup. To make tea, place the tea leaves in the gaiwan, add water, and leave to steep. The standard steeping times can be reduced because of the shape and size of the vessel – the domed lid allows good air flow and condensation, while the vessel, widening towards the top, allows the leaves plenty of room to release their flavours. Pour into a cup to serve, slightly tipping the lid so that the leaves remain inside, ready to be used for the next infusion. In China, some people drink directly from the gaiwan, leaves and all.

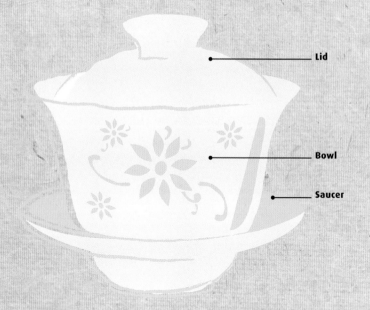

Lid

Bowl

Saucer

DOUBLE-WALLED GLASS CUP

Made of hand-blown glass, these cups keep the liquid hot by trapping air between layers of glass. Be careful with your first sip, though; the cup may be cool to the touch, but the water inside may be scalding.

Inner glass layer

Plunger

FRENCH PRESS

A coffee classic, the French press is also commonly used to infuse tea. The method of use is the same. Place the dry leaves in the press, pour the water over, leave for the recommended infusion time, and plunge. Use a light touch while plunging. The plunger should separate the leaves from the liquor, but not squeeze them enough to damage them, assuming that they will be used for another infusion. Pour all the tea out of the press when the infusion is ready to avoid over-steeping the leaves.

Release button

Built-in strainer

SMART INFUSERS

Usually made from BPA-free plastic, this infuser is the perfect size for single cups of tea. Place the leaves in the infuser, pour the water over, then place the infuser on top of a teapot or cup. Release the finished tea into the cup by pushing the button on the lid. Some infusers automatically release the tea when placed on the cup. They are certainly convenient, and favoured by tea rooms and tea shops, but no easier to clean than a teapot.

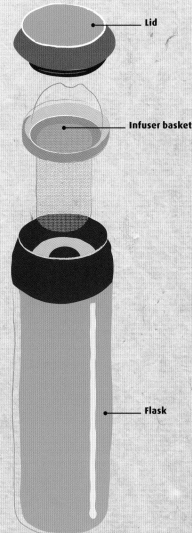

Lid

Infuser basket

Flask

TRAVEL FLASKS

There is an assortment of travel flasks available to make drinking on the go easy and convenient. Most flasks also have thermal insulation to keep the tea hot. Some have glass interiors, but most are made of stainless steel. The best ones have infuser baskets that nestle into the upper part of the flask. These are a mobile version of a teapot with an infuser. Place the dry leaves in the basket and pour some hot water through it. Tightly fasten the lid and invert the flask for infusion.

NEW WAYS TO INFUSE TEA

A number of innovative devices for infusing tea are now available. Some of them are simple and streamlined, others are eccentric, but they all produce a good cup of tea, and are well worth trying.

HOT INFUSERS

Traditionally, tea is infused with hot water, and leaves are processed with this in mind. There are now innovative alternatives to the conventional teapot that work equally well for infusion.

THE TEA SHAKER

This is a simple but brilliant concept. Composed of two compartments connected by a stainless steel filter, the tea shaker is similar to a classic hourglass. Place the tea leaves in the top compartment, add the hot water, and close the lid. Flip the device so it is upside down, and leave to infuse. After infusing for the required time, flip the device again and shake it from side to side to let the tea strain through the filter into the bottom compartment.

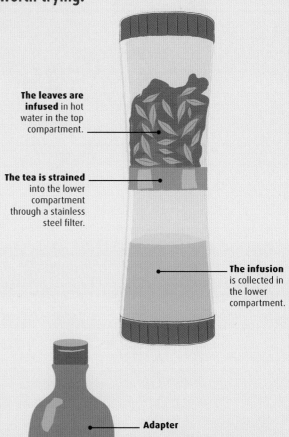

The leaves are **infused** in hot water in the top compartment.

The tea is strained into the lower compartment through a stainless steel filter.

The infusion is collected in the lower compartment.

Adapter

Built-in filter

The leaves are left to infuse in cold water.

COLD INFUSERS

These devices are designed for a long steep, and allow the tea leaves to release their flavours slowly. While it may seem counter-intuitive to the traditional practice of using hot water to draw out the tea's finest traits, cold infusion creates a lighter-bodied infusion, with a mellower, sweeter flavour. The method works particularly well with green and yellow teas, and is an inventive way of infusing Darjeelings.

SINGLE SERVE

This cold infuser comes in several shapes and is very easy to use. Place the dry leaves in the infuser and add cold water. Screw on the adapter with the built-in filter, and leave in the fridge to infuse for 2–3 hours. After that, pour the tea infusion through the adapter. Some infusers come with a removable infusion strainer, which holds the leaves, instead of a built-in filter. In such a case, remove the strainer before pouring.

INFUSER TOWER

The cold infuser tower has beakers and glass tubes, and it looks like a piece of laboratory equipment. Standing at 90–120cm (3–4ft) tall, it is too big to fit in the fridge. Place the leaves in the middle beaker. Pour cold water into the top beaker and add ice cubes to keep the infusion cold. The iced water will trickle through the leaves and follow a winding path to the bottom beaker. The whole process will take about 2 hours for white tea. Add another hour for green, yellow, and light oolongs, and increase to 4 hours for roasted oolongs. Pu'er and black teas take the longest to infuse, at about 5 hours.

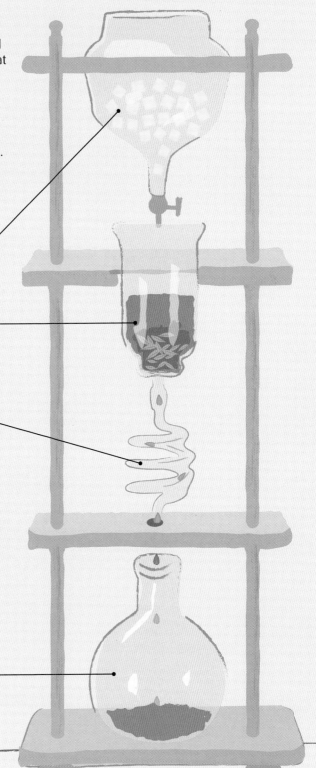

Cold water and ice cubes are placed in the top beaker.

The water trickles through the leaves in the middle beaker.

The infusion drips down the winding tubes.

The infused tea is collected in the lower beaker.

Use 50 per cent **more** dried leaf than you would use for a hot infusion. Cold infusion doesn't extract as many catechins or as much caffeine, which means the result will be sweeter.

COLD INFUSION REQUIRES LESS ENERGY AND THEREFORE HAS A SMALLER CARBON FOOTPRINT

BLENDING TEAS

The practice of blending began 400 years ago in the Fujian province of China, when loose-leaf tea replaced the solid, hard-to-blend brick tea, and jasmine and other flowers were added to enhance flavour and fragrance. While the classic blends remain popular, there are new blending styles that experiment with fruit and flowers. Practise the art of blending your own tea with these recipes.

There are two methods of blending tea: commerical blending and signature blending. Commercial blending involves using as many as 30–40 teas of various origins to create a consistent taste from season to season for the commercial tea bag industry. Master blenders taste hundreds of teas daily from all the tea-growing regions to create a dependable blend. The goal is to create the same flavours today that you had last year and the year before.

Signature blending, on the other hand, involves blending together several teas of different origins, usually with inclusions such as dried fruits, spices, or flowers. In a commercial kitchen, additional flavours and essences are usually sprayed on the tea leaves and they are placed in a blending drum for mixing, but you can blend your ingredients at home by stirring together in a bowl. All recipes are based on creating 200g (7oz) of blended tea.

CLASSIC BLENDS

Most tea lovers are familiar with these blends, and some of these classics have endured for centuries. Other than Genmaicha, all can be served with milk. Try the blend recipes given below, or experiment with the proportions to come up with your own signature blend.

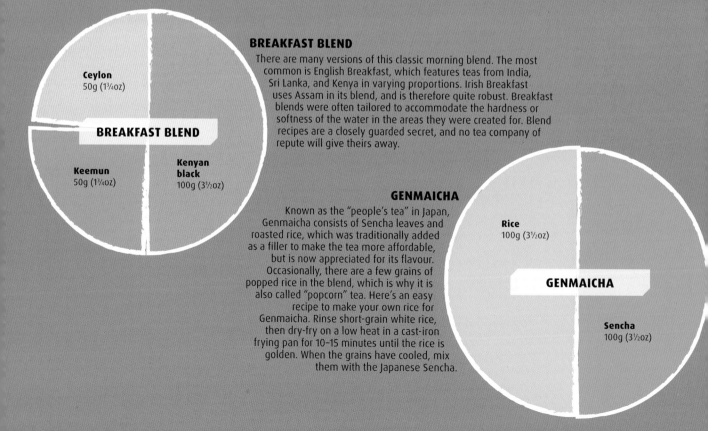

Ceylon
50g (1¾oz)

BREAKFAST BLEND

Keemun
50g (1¾oz)

Kenyan black
100g (3½oz)

BREAKFAST BLEND

There are many versions of this classic morning blend. The most common is English Breakfast, which features teas from India, Sri Lanka, and Kenya in varying proportions. Irish Breakfast uses Assam in its blend, and is therefore quite robust. Breakfast blends were often tailored to accommodate the hardness or softness of the water in the areas they were created for. Blend recipes are a closely guarded secret, and no tea company of repute will give theirs away.

GENMAICHA

Known as the "people's tea" in Japan, Genmaicha consists of Sencha leaves and roasted rice, which was traditionally added as a filler to make the tea more affordable, but is now appreciated for its flavour. Occasionally, there are a few grains of popped rice in the blend, which is why it is also called "popcorn" tea. Here's an easy recipe to make your own rice for Genmaicha. Rinse short-grain white rice, then dry-fry on a low heat in a cast-iron frying pan for 10–15 minutes until the rice is golden. When the grains have cooled, mix them with the Japanese Sencha.

Rice
100g (3½oz)

GENMAICHA

Sencha
100g (3½oz)

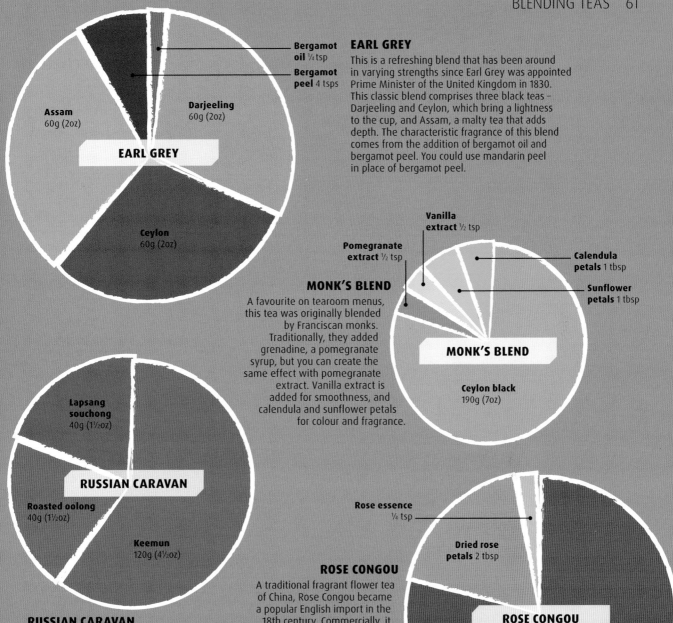

EARL GREY

This is a refreshing blend that has been around in varying strengths since Earl Grey was appointed Prime Minister of the United Kingdom in 1830. This classic blend comprises three black teas – Darjeeling and Ceylon, which bring a lightness to the cup, and Assam, a malty tea that adds depth. The characteristic fragrance of this blend comes from the addition of bergamot oil and bergamot peel. You could use mandarin peel in place of bergamot peel.

Bergamot oil ¼ tsp
Bergamot peel 4 tsps
Darjeeling 60g (2oz)
Assam 60g (2oz)
Ceylon 60g (2oz)

EARL GREY

Vanilla extract ½ tsp
Pomegranate extract ½ tsp
Calendula petals 1 tbsp
Sunflower petals 1 tbsp

MONK'S BLEND

A favourite on tearoom menus, this tea was originally blended by Franciscan monks. Traditionally, they added grenadine, a pomegranate syrup, but you can create the same effect with pomegranate extract. Vanilla extract is added for smoothness, and calendula and sunflower petals for colour and fragrance.

MONK'S BLEND

Ceylon black 190g (7oz)

RUSSIAN CARAVAN

This comforting blend is made from three Chinese black teas – Keemun, Lapsang Souchong, and roasted oolong – and pays homage to the camel caravans that delivered tea and other goods from China to Russia in the 19th century. The journey was long, usually lasting many months, and the tea was subjected to campfire smoke and exposed to the elements. This tea brings to mind the sweet smell of a wood fire, with just a little smokiness for those who don't like Lapsang Souchong's tarry taste on its own.

Lapsang souchong 40g (1½oz)

RUSSIAN CARAVAN

Roasted oolong 40g (1½oz)
Keemun 120g (4½oz)

ROSE CONGOU

A traditional fragrant flower tea of China, Rose Congou became a popular English import in the 18th century. Commercially, it is made by layering dried tea leaves and rose petals, until the flowers' oils are imparted to the tea. Often, rose petals are added for visual appeal. The sweetness of rose makes this a popular choice for afternoon tea. To make your own blend, add rose essence and dried rose petals to Chinese black congou tea, and allow to rest in an airtight container for several days.

Rose essence ¼ tsp
Dried rose petals 2 tbsp

ROSE CONGOU

Black congou 190g (7oz)

CONTEMPORARY BLENDS

The trend of adding fresh and dried fruit and flowers to tea has been growing in popularity over the last 5 years and there is a growing demand for these blends, characterized by strong, sweet, and fruity flavours. Usually named after pastries and puddings, these blends have become so popular that they now have their own category – "dessert teas". They are also at times known as "gateway teas", as people who may not initially enjoy tea on its own find them palatable. These teas are visually lovely, excellent when served cold, and work well as a liquid ingredient in baking.

It is not necessary to use a high-quality tea in these blends, as the other, more dominant flavours mask the subtleties of the tea leaf. The trick to making a good blend is to use ingredients that get along with one another, and do not fight for attention. A good rule of thumb is that if the ingredients work together as a dessert, they will probably work as a tea when a bold black tea is used as the base, although other types of tea can be used with the right ingredients. Here are some delicious dessert blends to try at home. Infuse them for the same length of time using the same temperature of water as recommended for their base tea.

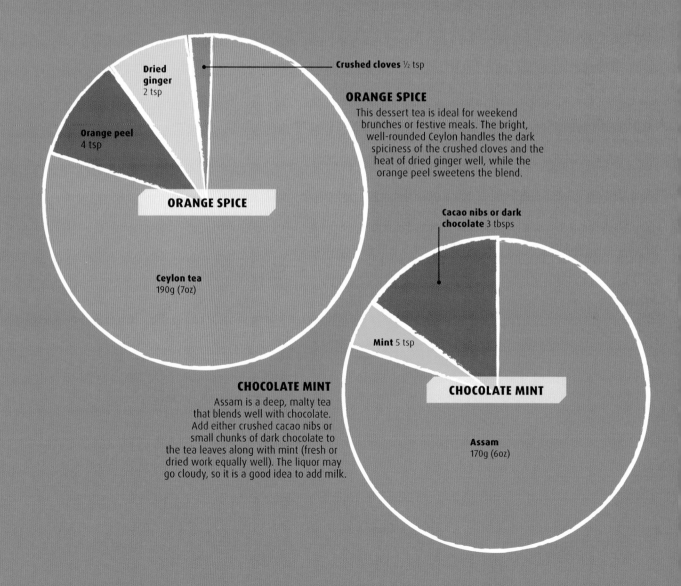

Crushed cloves ½ tsp

Dried ginger 2 tsp

Orange peel 4 tsp

ORANGE SPICE

Ceylon tea 190g (7oz)

ORANGE SPICE

This dessert tea is ideal for weekend brunches or festive meals. The bright, well-rounded Ceylon handles the dark spiciness of the crushed cloves and the heat of dried ginger well, while the orange peel sweetens the blend.

Cacao nibs or dark chocolate 3 tbsps

Mint 5 tsp

CHOCOLATE MINT

Assam 170g (6oz)

CHOCOLATE MINT

Assam is a deep, malty tea that blends well with chocolate. Add either crushed cacao nibs or small chunks of dark chocolate to the tea leaves along with mint (fresh or dried work equally well). The liquor may go cloudy, so it is a good idea to add milk.

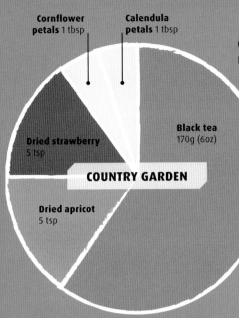

Cornflower petals 1 tbsp

Calendula petals 1 tbsp

Dried strawberry 5 tsp

Black tea 170g (6oz)

COUNTRY GARDEN

Dried apricot 5 tsp

COUNTRY GARDEN

Not only does this blend taste good, it also looks pretty and smells wonderful. The cornflower and calendula flowers evoke a summer garden, while the dried apricot and strawberry are reminiscent of orchards. The black tea anchors these flavours, keeping the sweetness and fruitiness in check.

Desiccated coconut 5 tsp

Lemongrass 1 tbsp

Gunpowder green 170g (6oz)

TROPICAL PARADISE

Dried mango pieces 4 tbsp

TROPICAL PARADISE

Green tea blends are best made with varieties like Gunpowder Green or other low-grade leaves. The tea should be considered an ingredient rather than a base as it does not stand out on its own, but makes a good addition to the mix nonetheless. This tropical blend of dried lemongrass, dried mango, and desiccated coconut is a crowd-pleaser that is both fun and refreshing.

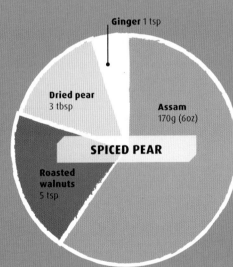

Ginger 1 tsp

Dried pear 3 tbsp

Assam 170g (6oz)

SPICED PEAR

Roasted walnuts 5 tsp

SPICED PEAR

Assam is a great choice in this nutty blend because it benefits from the sweetness of the dried pear. The roasted walnuts balance that sweetness while the ginger adds some spice. This tea stands up well to a splash of milk, if desired.

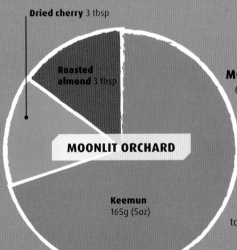

Dried cherry 3 tbsp

Roasted almond 3 tbsp

MOONLIT ORCHARD

Keemun 165g (5oz)

MOONLIT ORCHARD

Often called the "Burgundy of teas", Keemun is one of the richest and most satisfying black teas of China. The tea's own notes of black cherry make adding dried cherries an obvious choice. Chopped almonds balance the sweetness with their nutty flavour, while their natural oils add a smoothness to the blend.

TEAS OF
THE WORLD

HISTORY OF TEA

Since its discovery in Asia, tea has travelled the world, gaining popularity everywhere. Yet this beverage, known to revive mind and body, has had a tumultuous history, precipitating revolutions and causing wars.

Pu'er cakes

DISCOVERY OF TEA

It is believed that tea was discovered in China in 2737BCE by Emperor Shennong. While resting under a tea tree, he noticed the aroma from leaves that had fallen into a bubbling kettle. Intrigued by the fragrance, he took a sip and found the liquor refreshing.

ON THE MOVE

During the Tang Dynasty (618–907), Buddhist monks from Japan and Korea took Chinese tea seeds home and planted them. The monks in those countries nurtured a tea culture that is still in practice today.

Tang scholar
Lu Yu

TEA TIMELINE

2737BCE
Emperor Shennong discovers tea

760–762
The Tang scholar Lu Yu writes Cha Ching, The Book of Tea

828
Tea seeds reach Korea and are planted on Jiri mountain, near Hwagae village on the southern tip of Korea

420CE
Buddhist monks use tea leaves during meditation

618–907
The ancient Tea Horse Road, established during the Tang Dynasty, links the tea-producing areas of Yunnan with tea-consuming regions across China and Tibet

CULTIVATION

By 420CE, Zen Buddhist monks in China were using tea leaves to stay focused during their meditations. They grew tea plants near the monasteries, processed the tea into cakes, and sold it to locals. In time, farmers learnt to grow and process tea, and tea drinking became a part of daily life.

TRADE ROUTES

The Tea Horse Road, shown here in red, was established to connect China to Mongolia and Tibet. The Chinese used this route to barter tea (pressed into cakes) in exchange for strong horses, which they needed for transportation and warfare.

Tibet

CHINA

Sichuan

Yunnan

MONGOL INVASION

The Mongols invaded China in 1271, and established the Yuan dynasty (1271–1368). As the Mongols were not interested in the refined style of Chinese tea culture, preferring their own rustic form of preparation, indigenous Chinese tea culture started to disappear. Once the Ming Dynasty (1368–1644) came to power after the Mongols, tea processing styles evolved from pressed brick form to loose leaf.

MONGOLIAN TEA
The salty yak butter tea was, and still is, an essential element of the Mongolian diet.

1271
The Mongols invade China and Song dynasty tea traditions are lost

1590s
Portuguese missionary priests send letters home from China describing tea

1610
The Portuguese start to import tea from China

1619
The Dutch set up port in Batavia (now Jakarta), Indonesia to import tea and export it throughout Europe

1658
An advert in a London newspaper announces the availability of tea, known at the time as the "China drink", in a London coffee house. Only small amounts of tea are available in Britain at this time

1664
The East India Company begins to import tea from China into Britain via Java

TEA CRAZE

In the 16th century, the Portuguese were the first Europeans to drink tea, but it was the Dutch who made it popular. The Dutch became the largest importers of tea, and traded with other European countries. Due to its high price it was a drink exclusively for the wealthy.

EAST INDIA COMPANY

Formed in 1600 as a private company, the British East India Company (EIC) grew to be an all-powerful monopoly controlling half the world's trade. Although they began importing all of Britain's tea from China, they would go on to cultivate their own tea-growing source to supply Britain and its colonies.

Assam tea

BRAGANZA DOWRY

In 1662, the Portuguese princess Catherine of Braganza married the English king, Charles II. Her considerable dowry included chests of tea, already a popular drink among the Portugese nobility, as well as the the port of Bombay, which would become the EIC's trading headquarters in the Far East, allowing them to export tea all around the world. At this time, tea was not widely consumed in England, but Queen Catherine's fondness for the drink improved its popularity at court.

RUSSIAN TEA

Tea was introduced to Russia in 1638, but it was only after the Tea Camel Road was established that the Russians enjoyed a steady supply.

WHAT'S IN A NAME?

Since Europeans traded with tea merchants who spoke the Amoy dialect of China, they adopted their word "tay" for tea. This became "tea" in English, "thé" in French, "thee" in Dutch, and "tee" in German.

1662
Charles II, King of England, marries Portuguese princess Catherine of Braganza and tea drinking becomes popular among the British nobility

1689
The Tea Camel Road connects Russia and Mongolia, via Siberia, boosting tea trade between the countries

1676
The rise in popularity of tea in Britain leads King Charles II to introduce a 119 per cent taxation on tea

1773
Dissatisfaction over taxation in the American colonies leads to the "Boston Tea Party", in which a shipment of tea is dumped into the harbour

BRITISH COLONIES

Tea was enjoyed in the British colonies in North America, although it was highly taxed. To protest the British policy of taxation without representation, American colonists dumped a shipment of tea into Boston Harbour on 16th December 1773. The "Boston Tea Party" precipitated the American Revolution (1775–1783).

THE SMUGGLING TRADE

The high taxation on tea in Britain led to a thriving trade in tea smuggling. Tea was smuggled in to Britain from Europe via the Channel Islands and the Isle of Man. Although smuggling was widespread in the early 18th century, individual smugglers operated on a very small scale using small boats, sometimes even rowing boats, to bring fewer than 60 chests of tea to shore at a time.

INFILTRATING CHINA

Despite the discovery of indigenous tea plants in India, the EIC preferred the Chinese tea plant (var. *sinensis*). The *sinensis* variety proved to be better stock than the *assamica* variety because it could withstand the cooler weather and higher altitudes of Darjeeling. Botanist Robert Fortune was sent to obtain cuttings, seeds, and knowledge from China's inner provinces. During his trip from 1848–1851, Fortune shipped seeds and seedlings to India.

Chinese gaiwan

OPIUM WARS

While British tea gardens in India were being established the EIC continued to trade with China. The EIC sold opium, grown in India, to the Chinese in exchange for silver that they would then use to purchase tea. By the 1820s, opium addiction in China was widespread, which led the Chinese government to make smoking opium illegal. Since the opium trade went on despite these bans, two Opium Wars were fought between China and Britain, in the years between 1839 and 1860.

1778
Naturalist Joseph Banks recommends to the British government that tea be grown in northeast India

1823
Indigenous tea plants of the *assamica* variety are discovered in Assam, India

1837
America starts to trade directly with China

1839–1860
Opium wars

1784
British Prime Minister William Pitt reduces the tax on tea from 119 per cent to 12.5 per cent, making it more affordable for the working classes

1835
First cultivated tea plants grown in Assam using cuttings from indigenous var. *assamica* plants

1838
A small harvest of tea from Assam is sent to London for review

TEA FOR THE MASSES

During most of the 18th century in Britain, tea was priced out of reach of the working classes, but when the government reduced the duty on tea in 1784 they effectively ended tea smuggling and made tea affordable for most people.

The working class drank a low grade of tea and incorporated it into their daily meal, serving it with bread, butter, and cheese. Tea was drunk instead of ale, the popular drink of the time, so the health and mental alertness of the population improved.

TEA PLANTING IN INDIA

Long delivery times, high prices, and trade imbalances convinced the EIC that in order to have a steady source of tea they must begin to grow it in India. The first cultivated plants were grown in Assam, India, in 1835, although it would be more than a decade before tea was harvested on a large scale. By the 1870s, privately owned tea gardens expanded throughout Assam and Darjeeling, providing Britain with a cheaper, and more abundant, source of tea than the Chinese had been able to.

PORCELAIN

Craftsmen in Europe had perfected the porcelain-making process in the mid-18th century, and by the mid-19th century, bone china studios in Europe and England experienced a boom in business as they tried to keep up with demand for afternoon tea sets.

Darjeeling tea

BONE CHINA
Fine bone china cups and saucers had gilded edges to catch the lamp light in the evenings.

THE SUEZ CANAL

The Suez Canal opened in 1869, making the passage of steam ships from tea-producing countries in the East to Europe and North America economically viable where it had not been before. Passage was swift in these larger, faster steamships, so for the first time ever the Western market could drink fresh tea.

1840
First, unsuccessful, attempt by the British to grow tea in Ceylon (Sri Lanka)

1869
The Suez canal opens, and steamships are able to cut costs and time on trips to Asia. With coffee crop failure in Ceylon, tea planting begins in earnest

1840s
Clipper ships speed the delivery of tea to America

1869
The British start growing tea in Sri Lanka. The ready supply of tea leads to a dramatic fall in prices

1872
The first steam-powered rolling machines are used in Assam, reducing the time and cost of tea production

TEA AT SEA

In the first half of the century, ships had to sail around Africa's Cape of Good Hope to reach Britain and the USA. The newly invented clipper ship's low, sleek design and square rigged sails helped it travel at up to 20 knots per hour, bringing cargoes of tea to port in half the time of older vessels. The Cutty Sark, one of the last merchant ships to be built, carried tea until 1877.

INDIAN TEAS

In the second half of the 19th century, tea plantations prospered in India, and new land was cleared every year during Queen Victoria's reign (1837–1901). India produced excellent black teas that were in demand in Europe, Australia, and North America.

Clipper ship

TEA BLOCK
Before WWII, Chinese and Japanese green teas accounted for 40 per cent of all tea consumed in North America.

THE TEA BREAK

With the Industrial Revolution in full swing in the late 19th century, factory workers had to endure long shifts. Employers began providing free tea to their workers for mid-morning and afternoon breaks; this custom came to be known as the "tea break". In time, household servants began to be given tea allowances.

WORLD WAR II

Tea played a key role in boosting British morale during WWII. Although tea was rationed to 56g (2oz) per person, per week for civilians, extra was given to troops and those working in the emergency services.

As shipping lanes to North America were blocked as a result of the war, only black tea could be shipped across the Atlantic. By the end of the war, the North Americans had stopped drinking green tea altogether, and would only take it up again much later.

1908
Thomas Sullivan, a New York tea merchant, sends samples of tea to customers in silk pouches, inadvertently inventing the tea bag

1939–1945
World War II sees tea rationed and important trade routes for tea blocked

1960S–TODAY
Tea popularity continues to rise, making tea the second most widely consumed drink in the world, after water

1910
Indonesia begins to cultivate tea

1920
Tea bags are developed for the commercial market

1957
The Rotorvane machine is invented, making tea production more efficient

AFTERNOON TEA

By the end of the 19th century, afternoon tea had become a ritual in England, both with the aristocracy and with the middle classes.

Ladies entertained their close friends for tea at home wearing specially made tea gowns, which were informal flowing dresses worn without a corset. Tea shops opened on the high street and became the meeting place for the early suffragette movement.

TEA PLANTATION
Tea flourishes in Munnar in the southern state of Kerala at elevations of 1,600m (5,200ft).

AFTERNOON TEA

This quintessentially British custom, which began as a light afternoon snack, has evolved into an indulgent meal, winning fans worldwide. The classic afternoon tea is now being adapted to suit regional palates.

THE ORIGINS

The custom of afternoon tea came into practice in the 1840s, when gas-lighting was introduced in British upper class homes and it became possible, and fashionable, to take supper later in the evening. It was usual at the time to eat only two meals per day – breakfast and supper – so one influential aristocrat, the Duchess of Bedford, began to take tea with some light snacks at around 4pm to tide her over until supper. Over time, the Duchess began to invite her friends to take tea with her in her rooms at Woburn Abbey, Bedfordshire. Soon, this boudoir meal for aristocratic ladies evolved into a social custom practised in drawing rooms throughout the country, as well as in the British colonies.

Afternoon tea gave rise to increased demand for bone china tea sets and porcelain manufacturing all over the world thrived as a result. In North America, the custom reached its zenith in the 1950s, when Emily Post, an American author, wrote an essay on proper etiquette at tea.

Traditionally enjoyed in the late afternoon, tea is now taken between 2pm and 5pm and can replace both lunch and dinner. In recent years, it has seen a resurgence in interest, with hotels, cafés, and tea shops around the world offering themed afternoon teas with sweets and savouries.

TEA ETIQUETTE

Afternoon tea is so ingrained in British culture that everyone has their own idea of what is correct. Among the points of debate are the right way to eat a scone – whether to slice it or break it at its natural splitting point; the order in which you spread the clotted cream – before the jam, as per Cornish custom, or after, as done in Devon; whether to pour milk into the tea, or the tea into the milk, and so on.

Traditionally, a rich black tea, such as Darjeeing or Assam is served for afternoon tea. Afternoon blends and classic signature blends, such as Earl Grey, are also popular. Tea is always offered with a choice of milk or lemon and sugar. It is also customary to offer a variety of small crustless sandwiches, such as cucumber or smoked salmon with cream cheese, along with a sweet course of scones with jam and clotted cream, and pastries are served alongside the tea.

Today, venues offering afternoon tea are moving towards a more varied tea menu to complement the savouries and pastries on offer. A good selection of teas from around the world is usually available, including Japanese and Chinese greens, oolongs, custom blended teas, and fruit or herbal infusions. It's also quite common to start an afternoon tea with a glass of Champagne. There are many variations on the food served at afternoon tea depending on where you are in the world. You could have dim sum, fresh seafood, and hors d'oeuvres, in addition to macarons, cupcakes, and cakes.

MILK FIRST

There are many advantages to putting the milk into the teacup first. It was thought that the cold milk helped lower the temperature of the hot tea and, thus, protected the delicate bone china cups. But it is much more practical, and polite, for the host to serve the tea and let the guest add milk or sugar to their taste.

Although seemingly the epitome of British tea culture, afternoon tea is usually enjoyed as an occasional indulgence or to celebrate a special event, rather than an everyday occurrence.

CHINA

A country of mountainous tea regions, China invented tea drinking thousands of years ago and everything we now know about growing tea was first learned from the Chinese.

China is the world's largest tea producer but, as most is consumed domestically, relatively little is available for export. This has driven adventurous tea retailers in the West to develop close ties with Chinese tea growers to obtain premium teas for their customers.

China produces the greatest variety of teas of anywhere in the world and its tea makers are extremely knowledgeable about tea growing and production, largely because they have been manufacturing tea for over 4,000 years. Tea is still mostly plucked by hand and only produced using the orthodox method (see p21). Manufacturers may deviate from the usual production steps to create their own unique style of tea, which is often the case with small productions of green tea.

Although many Chinese producers are only associated with particular teas from their region, many are experimenting with other teas, for example, creating black (red) teas from cultivars that are usually made into green tea, or growing the Japanese Yabukita cultivar destined for Matcha production.

ASIA

Anji Bai Cha

CHINA KEY FACTS

PERCENTAGE OF WORLD PRODUCTION 36.8%

ELEVATION: MEDIUM TO HIGH

OTHER TEA-PRODUCING PROVINCES: ANHUI GUANGDONG, HUBEI

WORLD RANKING AS A PRODUCER: WORLD'S LARGEST TEA PRODUCER

MAIN TYPES: GREEN, OOLONG, WHITE, BLACK, PU'ER, YELLOW

HARVEST: MARCH–MAY

Anji Bai Cha is a green tea from Anji county in the Zhejiang province. Although "Bai" means "white" in Chinese, the tea is named after the light colour of its unplucked leaf.

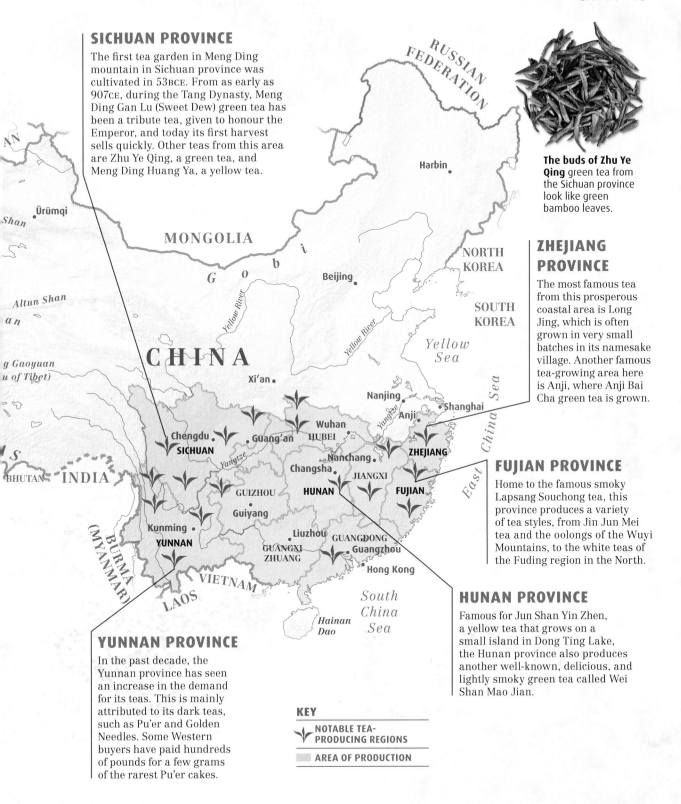

SICHUAN PROVINCE

The first tea garden in Meng Ding mountain in Sichuan province was cultivated in 53BCE. From as early as 907CE, during the Tang Dynasty, Meng Ding Gan Lu (Sweet Dew) green tea has been a tribute tea, given to honour the Emperor, and today its first harvest sells quickly. Other teas from this area are Zhu Ye Qing, a green tea, and Meng Ding Huang Ya, a yellow tea.

The buds of Zhu Ye Qing green tea from the Sichuan province look like green bamboo leaves.

ZHEJIANG PROVINCE

The most famous tea from this prosperous coastal area is Long Jing, which is often grown in very small batches in its namesake village. Another famous tea-growing area here is Anji, where Anji Bai Cha green tea is grown.

FUJIAN PROVINCE

Home to the famous smoky Lapsang Souchong tea, this province produces a variety of tea styles, from Jin Jun Mei tea and the oolongs of the Wuyi Mountains, to the white teas of the Fuding region in the North.

HUNAN PROVINCE

Famous for Jun Shan Yin Zhen, a yellow tea that grows on a small island in Dong Ting Lake, the Hunan province also produces another well-known, delicious, and lightly smoky green tea called Wei Shan Mao Jian.

YUNNAN PROVINCE

In the past decade, the Yunnan province has seen an increase in the demand for its teas. This is mainly attributed to its dark teas, such as Pu'er and Golden Needles. Some Western buyers have paid hundreds of pounds for a few grams of the rarest Pu'er cakes.

KEY

NOTABLE TEA-PRODUCING REGIONS

AREA OF PRODUCTION

CHINESE TEA CULTURE

Tea has been highly valued in Chinese life for thousands of years. Through the centuries, the culture and customs surrounding tea evolved into an art form. To the Chinese, tea was not only a tonic and medicine, it also had the ability to inspire creativity.

THE ANCIENT PAST

For over 4,000 years, tea was cultivated and consumed only in China. Then, after trade started along the Silk Road and Tea Horse Road (named after the main goods sold on these roads), areas near the Chinese border were introduced to tea. Although tea drinking had been part of Chinese life since the Han dynasty (206BCE–220CE), it was only under the Tang and Song dynasties (618–907CE and 960–1279CE) that elaborate ceremonies, such as Gongfu Cha (see pp78–83), came into practice. Lu Yu, a Tang dynasty scholar wrote a book called *Cha Ching* (The Classic of Tea). This detailed guide to tea planting, harvesting, and preparation was a turning point in tea history and was responsible for tea achieving cultural status in Chinese life.

TEA HOUSES

Beginning in the Tang dynasty, people of all classes gathered at "tea houses", which sold tea and refreshments, to discuss recent events and to socialize. They were often set on or near water, so that patrons could watch koi fish swimming beneath them and listen to the running water, which added to the beauty of the whole experience.

Tea houses became centres of social life where art was displayed, poetry, music, and calligraphy enjoyed, and even plays staged. During the Qing dynasty (1644–1912CE), operas depicting aspects of life in the tea hills became popular and were performed regularly. One of these, the Gannan Tea Picking Opera of Jiangxi province, has been performed for over 300 years, and features songs sung by tea pickers in the fields to pass the time.

BRICK TEA
Compressing tea leaves into bricks, like this one, made them less susceptible to physical damage along trade routes.

BAMBOO CASES
In ancient China, tea leaves were often encased in bamboo to protect the tea on long journeys along the tea-trading routes.

TRIBUTE TEA

In ancient China, every emperor expected tea leaves from the first harvest of the most highly valued gardens to be given to him as a "tribute". This practice benefited growers and increased sales of teas that had received the emperor's endorsement.

The tradition of producing "tribute teas" has evolved into the current practice in China of celebrating 10 famous teas each year. The list rarely changes from year to year, featuring mostly green teas, a few oolongs, and a black tea.

THE MODERN AGE

After the communist revolution in 1949, China isolated itself from the outside world, closing its doors for business and tourism to foreigners. This inadvertently helped to preserve traditional tea recipes and production processes. However, when the Cultural Revolution of the 1960s and 1970s swept the country, cultural artefacts and historic sites were lost in the attempt to "purge" the country of non-communist influences. While it is hard to estimate how this affected tea culture in particular, the country's recent interest in its rich past includes a resurgence in tea drinking.

ORNATE FANS
Women and men used beautifully decorated fans to cool themselves while enjoying tea.

CHINA'S TEA RENAISSANCE

Tea remains an important part of life in China. Taxi drivers have their ubiquitous jar of green tea in the cup holder of their cabs; there are schools that teach girls the fine art of presenting tea, so that they can take it up as a profession in China's many tea houses. Chinese tea producers are developing new black teas (known in China as "red teas") to appeal to the Western palate. In 2006, Jin Jun Mei, a new type of Lapsang Souchong from Wuyi, was introduced, and has since become quite sought after.

Tea tourism has also become popular, with enthusiasts visiting the tea cliffs of the Wuyi Mountains in Fujian province; the West Lake area of Hangzhou in Zhejiang province; or exploring the many tea-themed boutique hotels and restaurants of Lijiang in Yunnan province. Hong Kong draws many enthusiasts, too, as much for its famous milk tea (see the recipe on p176), as for Flagstaff House. Once the residence of the commander of the British forces, it now houses a teaware museum boasting the world's oldest surviving teapot.

PU'ER TEA
Pu'er tea was pressed into cakes and wrapped in rice paper.

BUDDHIST MONKS WERE THE FIRST TO CULTIVATE TEA AND SPREAD THIS KNOWLEDGE

CHINESE GONGFU CHA

A celebration of the process as much as the product, the Gongfu Cha ceremony pays homage to the time and effort required to prepare a good cup of tea. A variety of teaware is used, ranging from decorative porcelain to clay, each with a specific function.

"Gongfu" is the traditional Chinese method of tea preparation. "Gongfu" translates as "time" or "effort", while "cha" translates as "tea". The ceremony involves great skill and is mostly performed by women, whose choreographed hand movements are carefully timed to the steeping of the leaves and the eventual readiness of the tea. Gongfu Cha is most often performed using the lightly oxidized oolong Tie Guan Yin (Iron Goddess of Mercy), although any high quality tea can be used.

There are two regional styles of Gongfu Cha: the more modest ceremony, from Chaoshan in the Guangdong province, which distributes the tea directly into the cups; and the other ritual from the Wuyi mountains of Fujian, which uses the chahai, or fairness cup, to hold the prepared tea before distributing it evenly among the cups.

Yixing teapots are the most popular choice for preparing tea for the ceremony. Made of unglazed clay, they absorb the aromas of the tea and, as such, are often reserved for just one type of tea. A combination of porcelain and glass teaware may be used for the serving vessels.

YIXING CLAY TEAPOT
This unglazed teapot, made from regional clay from Yixing, in the Jiangsu province, is rinsed with hot water to clean and warm it before tea leaves are added.

TEA STRAINER
Used to catch the leaves while pouring the tea into tea cups.

SCOOP
Used to add tea leaves to the pot.

NOSING CUP
This small cup is used to enjoy the aroma of the tea before it is consumed.

TEA PET
This small figurine, made of Zisha clay and depicting an animal or mythical creature, changes colour when hot water is poured over it. It is believed to bring good fortune to the tea ceremony.

TASTING CUP
Tea from the nosing cup is emptied into the tasting cup for the guest to drink.

WASTE WATER BOWL
This large bowl is used to collect waste water emptied from tea cups.

TONGS
Used to pick up the hot nosing and tasting cups when they are being warmed and rinsed.

TEAPOT PICK
Dislodges tea leaves from the spout of the teapot.

FAIRNESS CUP
Tea is poured from the fairness cup, or "chahai" to ensure an even distribution.

SPOON
A long tea spoon for scraping and removing wet leaves from the teapot.

TEA BOAT
A decorative wooden, or bamboo, tray on which tea is prepared. It has slats to drain waste water, and a drawer inside to catch any overflow.

FUNNEL
Placed in the teapot to guide the dry leaves into the pot, the funnel helps ensure that no tea leaves are wasted.

SERVING TRAY
Used to present the tasting and nosing cups to the guests.

TEA CLOTH
During the ceremony, the cloth is folded and used for wiping and holding the teaware.

PERFORMING GONGFU CHA

The Fujianese style of the Gongfu Cha tea ceremony engages both the host and the guests with its intricate movements. The chahai, or "fairness cup", used for equal distribution of the tea, is unique to this ritual of preparing tea.

1 **The host pours water**, heated to 85°C (185°F), into and over the Yixing teapot in slow circular motions to warm it up, then pours the water from the teapot into the fairness cup.

2 **The water is poured from the fairness cup** into the nosing and tasting cups, in sweeping back and forth motions, to warm them. Tongs are later used to empty the cups.

3 **Leaves are measured using the scoop** and placed into the teapot using the wooden funnel. The teapot is shaken lightly to awaken the leaves.

4 **The teapot is filled with heated water** from a height until it is overflowing. The lid is then placed on the teapot in a circular sliding motion (see inset).

5 **The tea is immediately poured** into the fairness cup, then into the nosing and tasting cups to keep them warm. It is then poured over the tea pet (see inset), for good luck. This first steep is considered a rinse infusion and is used to further warm the vessels, before it is discarded.

6 **The tea leaves will begin to open.** For the first infusion after the rinse, hot water is poured into and onto the teapot, until it overflows. The lid is replaced, as before, and hot water is poured over to clean and warm the pot. The tea is left to infuse for at least 10 seconds.

7 **Tongs are then used** to empty the tasting and nosing cups of the rinse infusion. The tea in the fairness cup is poured into the waste water bowl.

8 **The underside of the teapot is dried** with a soft cloth, and the tea is poured into the fairness cup through the tea strainer.

9 **The tea is then poured from the fairness cup** into the nosing cups, in a sweeping back and forth motion, until full, but not overflowing.

10 **The host places the tasting cup** over the nosing cup in an inverted position and carefully flips it over to transfer the tea to the tasting cup.

11 **Holding the nosing cup in place**, the tasting cup is placed on the serving tray. The nosing cup is then lifted off the tasting cup.

12 **The tasting cup is presented to the guest**, along with the nosing cup. The host then begins the second infusion, adding 5 seconds to the infusion time.

THE ROLE OF THE GUEST
Before drinking from the tasting cup, the guest lifts the nosing cup to smell the aroma of the tea and, on tasting, comments on the flavours.

INDIA

Traditionally, India is known for its malty Assams and prized Darjeelings. Now the country is experimenting with growing different types of tea, such as Nilgiri Frost and Darjeeling Green.

Tea grown in India accounts for around 22 per cent of the world's tea production. Most of the tea grown in India is consumed within the country, with 20 per cent being exported globally. In the early 1900s Indian tea was mostly consumed by upper- and middle-class Indians, with the vast majority of tea being exported to the West. It wasn't until the advent of the CTC process (see p21) in the 1950s that Indian tea became more affordable for the wider domestic market.

Tea cultivation began in earnest in India in the 19th century to supply the British with their own source of their favourite beverage.

The East India Company arranged to have seeds and plants smuggled from China, which were bred with local Assam plants. The cool climate in Darjeeling allowed the Chinese plants to flourish.

Although famed for its Darjeelings and Assams, today India is trying to promote its lesser-known teas, such as Nilgiri Frost, which is picked in late January or February, when the temperatures suddenly drop below freezing, producing very fragrant tea. Darjeeling tea gardens are also growing and producing different varieties of white and green tea, which have fresh and sweet flavours.

PLANTATIONS IN MUNNAR
There are more than 50 tea plantations in and around the small hill station of Munnar in Kerala, covering an area of 3,000 hectares (7,413 acres).

INDIA KEY FACTS

PERCENTAGE OF WORLD PRODUCTION: 22.3%

TEA TYPES: BLACK, GREEN, WHITE

HARVEST: MAY–OCTOBER IN THE NORTH; YEAR-ROUND IN THE SOUTH

FAMOUS FOR: BEING THE FIRST CULTIVATED TEA REGION IN THE BRITISH EMPIRE

ELEVATION: LOW–HIGH

INDIA IS THE SECOND LARGEST PRODUCER OF TEA IN THE WORLD

SOUTH ASIA

KANGRA, HIMACHAL PRADESH

While the Kangra region mostly produces black tea, it also produces small amounts of green tea using traditional Chinese-style manufacturing methods.

SIKKIM

The Temi Estate in Sikkim, located north of Darjeeling, was planted with Darjeeling cultivars in the 1960s. The tea produced in this region has refreshing muscatel flavours and low astringency.

JAMMU & KASHMIR

Amritsar
KANGRA HIMACHAL PRADESH

PAKISTAN

PUNJAB

HARYANA

DELHI New Delhi

CHINA

HIMALAYAS

NEPAL

BHUTAN

SIKKIM
DARJEELING

ARUNACHAL PRADESH

ASSAM

NAGALAND

Thar Desert

UTTARAKHAND

Ganges

Jaipur

RAJASTHAN

Lucknow

UTTAR PRADESH

BIHAR

Ganges

MEGHALAYA

MANIPUR

BURMA (MYANMAR)

BANGLADESH

Brahmaputra

GUJARAT

Ahmadabad

Narmada

MADHYA PRADESH

JHARKHAND

WEST BENGAL

Kolkata (Calcutta)

TRIPURA

MIZORAM

INDIA

Nagpur

CHHATTISGARH

ODISHA

Bay of Bengal

Mumbai (Bombay)

MAHARASHTRA

TELANGANA
Hyderābād

Arabian Sea

Western Ghats

KARNATAKA

GOA

ANDHRA PRADESH

Eastern Ghats

NILGIRI

Tea is grown at very high elevations in the Nilgiri Hills of the Western Ghats of Tamil Nadu where temperatures are cool and the monsoon weather contributes to lush growth. This region is home to Nilgiri Frost black tea, as well as some green and white teas.

INDIAN OCEAN

Bengaluru (Bangalore)

Chennai (Madras)

NILGIRI

KERALA

TAMIL NADU

MUNNAR

SRI LANKA

MUNNAR, KERALA

Sitting at a high altitude in the southwestern state of Kerala, Munnar was a summer resort of the British in the colonial days. Tea plantations were established here as early as the 1870s, and teas produced here are similar in character to Nilgiri teas.

Nilgiri black tea, grown on the Western Ghats mountain range in Tamil Nadu, is well rounded in flavour and low in tannins.

KEY

NOTABLE TEA-PRODUCING REGIONS

AREA OF PRODUCTION

ASSAM

The Assam region of India benefits from rich soil and monsoon rains, making it the most productive tea-growing region in the world. Characterized by deep, bold flavours, Assam tea makes up approximately 50 per cent of India's total output of tea.

Located in the northeast corner of India on the low-lying alluvial flood plains of the Brahmaputra River Valley, Assam is a prime region for tea cultivation and produces mostly commodity tea using the CTC method (see p21) for the tea bag industry.

The rich soil is fed by floods during the monsoon season (May–October), and tea is picked from April to November, during the hottest and wettest season. Temperatures can reach 38°C (100°F) at this time of the year, simulating the conditions in a terrarium or green house. First flush Assam tea is harvested in April, while the second flush is picked from May to June and is most often used in black tea blends, such as East Frisian or afternoon blends. Some growers are turning to orthodox production (see p21) to create high-grade whole leaf for export at a higher price than commodity tea. As such, orthodox Assam tea is protected under Geographical Indication, which ensures that all tea carrying the name "Assam" has come from this region.

The Assam region operates on a different time from the rest of India – "Bagan Time", or "Tea Garden Time", sees clocks set one hour ahead of IST (Indian Standard Time), allowing workers to take advantage of an early sunrise.

INDIA

BRAHMAPUTRA RIVER VALLEY

The Brahmaputra River runs the full length of the state of Assam. This river valley is divided into four main tea-growing regions – Upper Assam, North Bank, Central Assam, and Lower Assam.

BHUT

Bongaiga

Dhubri

BANGLADESH

ASSAM KEY FACTS

PERCENTAGE OF WORLD PRODUCTION: **13%**

HARVEST: APRIL–NOVEMBER

MAIN TYPES: **BLACK CTC,** ORTHODOX BLACKS, GREEN

FAMOUS FOR: BEING THE **MOST PRODUCTIVE TEA-GROWING REGION** IN THE **WORLD**

ELEVATION: **LOW**

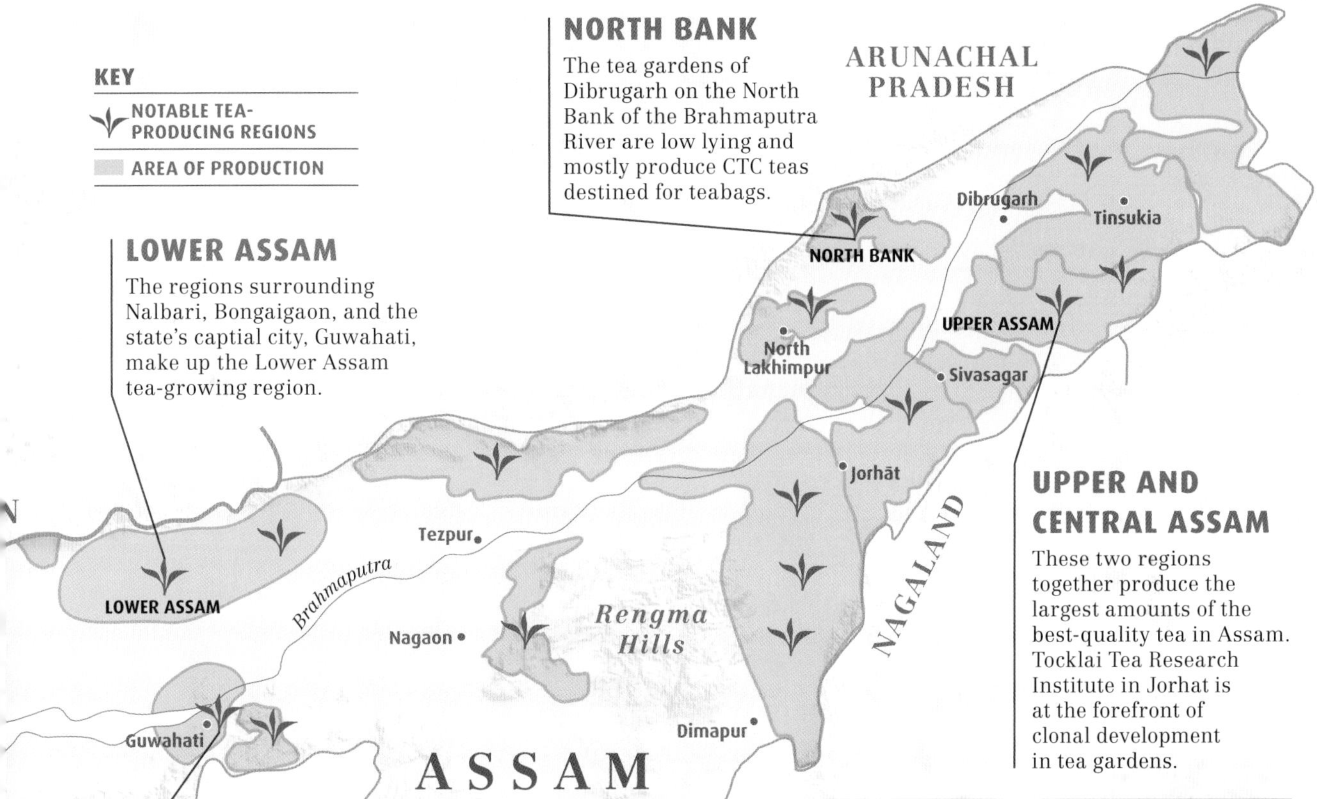

KEY

- NOTABLE TEA-PRODUCING REGIONS
- AREA OF PRODUCTION

NORTH BANK

The tea gardens of Dibrugarh on the North Bank of the Brahmaputra River are low lying and mostly produce CTC teas destined for teabags.

LOWER ASSAM

The regions surrounding Nalbari, Bongaigaon, and the state's captial city, Guwahati, make up the Lower Assam tea-growing region.

ARUNACHAL PRADESH

NORTH BANK

Dibrugarh

Tinsukia

UPPER ASSAM

North Lakhimpur

Sivasagar

Jorhāt

Tezpur

Rengma Hills

Nagaon

Dimapur

LOWER ASSAM

NAGALAND

Guwahati

Brahmaputra

A S S A M

MEGHALAYA

Barail Range

UPPER AND CENTRAL ASSAM

These two regions together produce the largest amounts of the best-quality tea in Assam. Tocklai Tea Research Institute in Jorhat is at the forefront of clonal development in tea gardens.

GUWAHATI

Most of the CTC tea produced in Assam goes to auction in Guwahati and is mostly bought for the domestic market.

MANIPUR

TRIPURA

MIZORAM

WILD DISCOVERY

The Assam tea plant (*Camellia sinensis* var. *assamica*) was first discovered growing wild in the hills of the Upper Assam region in 1823. It was later classified as a variety of *Camellia sinensis*, but has wider leaves than the *sinensis* variety.

Tea harvested during Assam's second flush is considered to have the best flavours because hot and wet growing conditions bring out the malty richness of the tea.

DARJEELING

The Darjeeling region of India may cover only 181sq km (70sq miles), but it produces one of the most famous teas in the world. Cool temperatures and high altitudes produce leaves with aromatic flavours that are highly acclaimed.

Located in the state of West Bengal in north India, Darjeeling sits at the edge of the Himalayas. A well-established tea-growing region, some of its 87 tea estates date back to the mid-1800s. Darjeeling produces only 1.13 per cent of India's total output of tea, but it is of such high quality that it is protected by Geographical Indication. This has, however, been difficult to enforce, and there are growers selling counterfeit Darjeelings, which have been padded with other Himalayan teas sourced from outside the designated Darjeeling region. The Tea Board of India has developed a trademark logo for Darjeeling to help buyers identify authentic tea from the region.

Var. *sinensis* is grown here along with some var. *assamica* hybrids. The high elevation, 1,000–2,100m (3,280–6,890ft), influences the flavour of the finished tea. The leaves grow very slowly because they are constantly shrouded in cool mist. During the growing season, the plants respond well to warm days and cool evenings. These conditions help to create intense flavours in the leaves.

HARVESTING THE LEAVES
In Darjeeling, female workers hand pluck the leaves over three harvesting seasons, with the first flush starting in mid-March.

DARJEELING KEY FACTS

PERCENTAGE OF WORLD PRODUCTION: 0.36%

MAIN TYPES:
BLACK, OOLONG, GREEN, WHITE

FAMOUS FOR:
GEOGRAPHICAL INDICATION AND DARJEELING TRADEMARK

HARVEST:
FIRST FLUSH
MARCH–APRIL
SECOND FLUSH
MAY–JUNE
AUTUMNAL FLUSH
OCTOBER–NOVEMBER

ELEVATION:
HIGH

Second flush
Darjeeling has layered flavours with distinct notes of muscat grape.

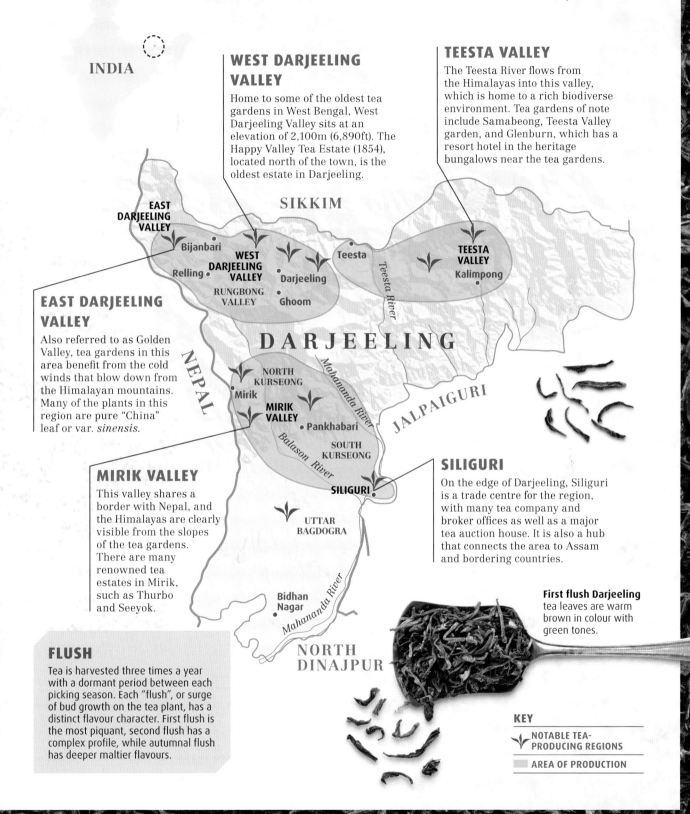

INDIA

WEST DARJEELING VALLEY

Home to some of the oldest tea gardens in West Bengal, West Darjeeling Valley sits at an elevation of 2,100m (6,890ft). The Happy Valley Tea Estate (1854), located north of the town, is the oldest estate in Darjeeling.

TEESTA VALLEY

The Teesta River flows from the Himalayas into this valley, which is home to a rich biodiverse environment. Tea gardens of note include Samabeong, Teesta Valley garden, and Glenburn, which has a resort hotel in the heritage bungalows near the tea gardens.

EAST DARJEELING VALLEY

SIKKIM

Bijanbari

WEST DARJEELING VALLEY

Relling

RUNGBONG VALLEY

Darjeeling

Ghoom

Teesta

TEESTA VALLEY

Kalimpong

Teesta River

EAST DARJEELING VALLEY

Also referred to as Golden Valley, tea gardens in this area benefit from the cold winds that blow down from the Himalayan mountains. Many of the plants in this region are pure "China" leaf or var. *sinensis*.

DARJEELING

NEPAL

Mahananda River

NORTH KURSEONG

Mirik

MIRIK VALLEY

Pankhabari

Balason River

SOUTH KURSEONG

JALPAIGURI

MIRIK VALLEY

This valley shares a border with Nepal, and the Himalayas are clearly visible from the slopes of the tea gardens. There are many renowned tea estates in Mirik, such as Thurbo and Seeyok.

SILIGURI

SILIGURI

On the edge of Darjeeling, Siliguri is a trade centre for the region, with many tea company and broker offices as well as a major tea auction house. It is also a hub that connects the area to Assam and bordering countries.

UTTAR BAGDOGRA

Bidhan Nagar

Mahananda River

NORTH DINAJPUR

First flush Darjeeling tea leaves are warm brown in colour with green tones.

FLUSH

Tea is harvested three times a year with a dormant period between each picking season. Each "flush", or surge of bud growth on the tea plant, has a distinct flavour character. First flush is the most piquant, second flush has a complex profile, while autumnal flush has deeper maltier flavours.

KEY

↓ NOTABLE TEA-PRODUCING REGIONS

▊ AREA OF PRODUCTION

INDIAN TEA CULTURE

The British began to cultivate tea in India in 1835. Since then, tea has become an integral part of the Indian culture and economy, and local customs and traditions have emerged around the beloved Indian chai.

TEA CULTIVATION

Tea had become a popular beverage in England by the 18th century, so to meet the increasing demand of the British, and break the Chinese monopoly, the British East India Company (EIC) smuggled tea seeds and skilled workers from China, and established tea gardens in the northern part of India. It wasn't until the mid-19th century that the newly cultivated tea plants in Darjeeling and Assam were harvested and India began to supply tea to England and the other British colonies.

THE BRITISH GRADING SYSTEM

To get a good price for the tea they were selling, the British introduced a grading system for black tea based on the appearance of orthodox tea leaves, with the unbroken and unblemished whole leaf being superior to the broken leaf. This system is followed to this day in India, Sri Lanka, and Kenya. It's common for the leaves to break into smaller pieces of varying sizes during processing, especially after they have been dried, as they can become quite brittle. Once the leaves have been sifted and graded, only dust and "fannings", or tiny pieces of leaf, are left. These are considered the lowest grade, but if they are the fannings from a superior tea crop, they can be used to create popular commercial black tea blends.

The British grading system is based only on the appearance and size of the leaf, and does not evaluate the flavour, aroma, or the taste of the liquor. Some grades refer to "flowery" traits, indicating the presence of a small leaf bud in the tea leaf, while others refer to "golden" or "orange", indicating the presence of golden tips on the tea leaf buds or the colour of the liquor.

WHOLE LEAF

SFTGFOP	Special Fine Tippy Golden Flowery Orange Pekoe (smallest whole leaf)
FTGFOP	Fine Tippy Golden Flowery Orange Pekoe
TGFOP	Tippy Golden Flowery Orange Pekoe
GFOP	Golden Flowery Orange Pekoe
FOP	Flowery Orange Pekoe
FP	Flowery Pekoe
OP	Orange Pekoe

BROKEN LEAF

GFBOP	Golden Flowery Broken Orange Pekoe
GBOP	Golden Broken Orange Pekoe
FBOP	Flowery Broken Orange Pekoe
BOP1	Broken Orange Pekoe One
BOP	Broken Orange Pekoe
BPS	Broken Pekoe Souchong

IN THE EARLY 1900s, ALMOST ALL OF THE TEA PRODUCED IN INDIA WAS BLACK TEA

CHAI

Despite tea cultivation beginning in India in the 1850s, the practice of taking tea, or chai, with milk and sugar became popular only in the latter half of the 19th century when British plantation owners introduced it to the masses. The rich creaminess of buffalo milk, traditionally used in India to make chai, complements the robustness of Indian teas, especially Assam. Although the high butterfat content in buffalo milk is preferred, any type of dairy-based milk can be used.

"Masalas", or aromatic spices, have always been a key component of Indian cuisine. Hot beverages made with masalas were traditionally drunk for medicinal purposes. During the late 19th century, a marriage of these spices with milky, sweet tea resulted in the rich and spicy beverage we now know as Masala Chai (see recipe on pp182–83).

CHAI BREAK
The sheer number of chai stalls occupying the streets of India is a clear indication of the popularity of the drink. Both office workers and labourers alike can be seen taking tea in stalls at all hours of the day.

KULLARHS

Chai wallahs, or tea vendors, make Masala Chai from scratch with their own blend of spices, low-quality black tea, milk, and sugar. The chai is poured from a height and often served in small, lightly fired clay cups known as "kullarhs". Hygienic and environmentally friendly, kullarhs are made of degradable clay and are discarded on the roadside after the chai has been consumed.

SPICED CHAI
Bursting with flavour and aroma, the Masala Chai's kick comes from an assortment of spices including cloves, cinnamon, cardamom, and ginger.

SRI LANKA

Formerly a British colony called Ceylon, this small and vibrant island nation is famed for the array of high-quality teas that it grows and produces using traditional methods.

Originally a coffee-growing nation, Sri Lanka switched to tea production in 1869, when a devastating blight infested the majority of its coffee plantations. Present day tea exports are still referred to as "Ceylon tea" despite the island reverting to its former name in 1972.

Tea is grown mostly in the central highlands of the country, and can be divided into three groups based on the elevation of the area where it is grown: high-grown; medium-grown; or low-grown. The country's two monsoon seasons affect each area differently, with changing wind patterns creating different micro-climates that give each area's tea its distinct character.

Although the country's tea industry suffered greatly through the years of civil war, it has recovered in recent years and now its bright, flavourful black teas and Ceylon Silver Tips white tea are enjoying good reviews worldwide. Over 1 million people are employed in the industry and tea leaves are still hand-picked.

SRI LANKAN TEA ESTATES
Deciduous trees are planted on the slopes to provide the tea plants with a few hours of shade per day.

SRI LANKA KEY FACTS

PERCENTAGE OF WORLD PRODUCTION: **7.4%**

FAMOUS FOR:
TEA GARDENS AND **BRITISH** STYLE TEAS

HARVEST:
DECEMBER–APRIL
WITH SOME AREAS HARVESTING YEAR ROUND

MAIN TYPES:
BLACK, WHITE

ELEVATION:
HIGH, MEDIUM, LOW

BLACK TEAS FROM RATNAPURA HAVE A DISTINCTIVE SWEETNESS

SOUTH
ASIA

DIMBULA

Dimbula is located in the Western Highland's mountainous region. Here, tea is grown at 1,000–1,700m (3,280–5,600ft), and is classified as high-grown tea. Teas from this region have a strong, rich, full-bodied flavour.

UVA

Located in the Eastern Highlands, this was one of the first areas to be planted. At elevations of 1,000–1,700m (3,280–5,600ft), Uva experiences a season of winds that dramatically affects the tea leaves. The buds close in reaction to the wind, and the plant is forced to preserve moisture. This creates a sweeter leaf and, as such, fetches a higher price.

KANDY

The first tea plantation in Kandy was started in 1867. At elevations of 750–1,200m (2,500–4,000ft), the teas here are medium-grown. Strong and robust, they are often used in tea blends, such as Earl Grey and English Breakfast.

NUWARA ELIYA

Located in the Central Highlands at an elevation of 2,000m (6,500ft), teas grown at Nuwara Eliya are considered high-grown. Tea buds develop more slowly at this elevation resulting in a sweet fruity taste. This region produces a silver-tipped white tea as well as traditional black tea.

Palk Strait

Palk Bay

SRI LANKA

Knuckles Range

Gulf of Mannar

Bay of Bengal

Matale

KANDY

Ampara

Inginiyagala

Colombo

NUWARA ELIYE   **DIMBULA**

UVA

Monaragala

Arugam Bay

Ratnapura

Kataragama

Galle

Yala

The tea industry accounts for 2 per cent of Sri Lanka's economy.

KEY

↴ NOTABLE TEA-PRODUCING REGIONS

▨ AREA OF PRODUCTION

TEA CUSTOMS AROUND THE WORLD

Tea recipes and traditions differ from country to country and region to region, and are shaped by diverse factors, such as geographical location, availability of ingredients, and dietary practices. The following three regions stand out for their unique tea-drinking rituals.

EAST FRISIA, GERMANY

Located on the northern coast of Germany and facing the North Sea, East Frisia's relative isolation has resulted in a unique tea culture.

Tea has been consumed in the region since the drink was introduced to Europe in the 17th century. By the 1800s, the East Frisians were making and preparing their own distinct blend, and the techniques practised have remained unchanged. Today, the annual per capita consumption of tea in East Frisia is 300 litres (634 pints) – among the highest in the world.

There are four local blenders – Bünting, Onno Behrends, Thiele, and Uwe Rolf – who buy their tea in Hamburg, the largest hub for tea importing in Europe. They carefully guard their recipes, but the strong black blends contain mostly second flush Assam leaves, with small amounts of Ceylon and Darjeeling.

The tea is prepared in a porcelain teapot using generous amounts of dry leaf to create a strong infusion. To serve, lumps of kluntjes, a type of rock sugar, are placed in small porcelain cups. The infusion is poured on top and double cream is added. The mixture is not stirred – the sugar melts slowly, sweetening subsequent cups, while the cream creates a "tea cloud" and slowly mixes in. Rich and malty in flavour, a fortifying measure of rum is added during the winter months.

TEA CUPS
East Frisian tea is served in small, often ornate, porcelain cups.

MONGOLIA

At the time of the Mongol Empire's invasion of China in the 13th century, the Mongols drank a tea called "suutei tsai", a strong, milky tea made with pressed black tea, water, milk, salt, and, occasionally, fried millet. During their time in China, the Mongols rejected Chinese tea culture in favour of their traditional salty black tea.

Tea supplemented the Mongol diet, which mostly consisted of dairy, meat, and grains. As water was scarce and, therefore, sacred to the Mongols, they did not drink it on its own, but used it to make their suutei tsai. Milk from the family's herd of cows, yaks, goats, mares, sheep, or camels was boiled together with tea, water, and salt, then ladled from a height into tea bowls.

Suutei tsai is still an essential part of Mongolian society. The tea is consumed frequently during the day and at various occasions, such as to seal business deals, welcome guests, or at family gatherings. It is considered rude to refuse an offer of suutei tsai.

TIBET

Tibet's association with tea can be traced back to the 13th century, when the Chinese traded tea for Tibetan horses along the famous Tea Horse Road. This treacherous network of caravan trails and mountain footpaths linked the Sichuan province in southwest China to Tibet. Although most of Tibet does not have the right terroir for growing tea, farmers in the region of Pemagul grow a small amount that is made into black brick tea. Tibetans still use this tea, little known and not widely available outside of Tibet, to make their distinctive yak butter tea, known as po cha.

Po cha is made by boiling a large amount of crushed brick tea in hot water for half a day to make a strong tea liquor. This tea liquor, along with yak milk, butter, and salt, is then poured into a dogmo, a long wooden churn, and churned and beaten until it is creamy, rich, and light in colour. The po cha is poured into a teapot, traditionally made of metal but now commonly made of ceramics, and then into large wooden or earthenware cups for drinking. It is customary for the drinker to sip the tea leisurely, allowing the host to top up the cup after every sip. While the salty po cha can be an acquired taste for visitors, Tibetans rely on the rich tea to provide them with the additional calories required to survive in the region's harsh climate and high elevations. Tibetan nomads are said to drink up to 40 cups of po cha a day.

IT IS USUAL
FOR EAST
FRISIANS TO
DRINK THREE
CUPS OF TEA
PER SITTING

PO CHA
This salty yak butter tea from Tibet is also enjoyed in Nepal, Bhutan, and the Himalayan regions of India.

JAPAN

With a tea history that can be traced back to the 12th century, Japan is best known for its green teas. Due to high domestic demand, Japan exports only about 3 per cent of its teas.

Tea was first brought to Japan around 805CE by Japanese monks returning from China. However, it was only in the 12th century that the tea plant began to thrive in the Uji area of the Kyoto prefecture. Tea is now mainly grown on two islands, Honshu and Kyushu, with the sea air lending marine and seaweed flavours to the tea. Nearly 75 per cent of the tea in Japan is grown using the Yabukita cultivar, which was developed in 1954 in the Shizuoka prefecture. Its leaves have a strong aroma and an intense flavour. This cultivar provides an abundant growth of leaves, can resist Japan's cool weather, and is suited to the island country's soil.

In Japan, the harvesting and processing of tea leaves are mechanized due to high labour costs. Tall electric fans are a common sight in Japanese tea gardens. These are strategically placed throughout the gardens in order to moderate temperatures, helping to prevent frost in cold spring weather by pushing warm air down towards the tender new growth of the plants.

Sencha, with its needle-shaped leaves, is the most widely produced green tea in Japan, accounting for nearly 80 per cent of the country's total tea production.

JAPAN KEY FACTS

PERCENTAGE OF WORLD PRODUCTION: **1.9%**

MAIN TYPE: GREEN

FAMOUS FOR: GYOKURO, SENCHA, GENMAICHA, MATCHA

ELEVATION: LOW

HARVEST: APRIL–OCTOBER

SUWA NO CHAYA TEA HOUSE
This tea house from the Edo period (1603–1868) was moved to its present location in the Imperial Palace grounds in 1912. It is built in the formal and traditional Japanese style.

ASIA

Gyokuro tea is the highest quality of shaded green tea. "Gyokuro" translates to "jade dew", indicating the colour of the pale green infusion.

Hokkaido

Sapporo

PACIFIC OCEAN

THE FIRST TEA OF THE NEW SEASON'S HARVEST IS CALLED SHINCHA

Sendai

Sado

Sea of Japan

JAPAN

Hida Mts

KYOTO PREFECTURE

Kyoto is an ancient tea-growing area, and the town of Uji is a key area for the production of Gyokuro and Matcha (both shaded for two weeks before harvest). Other areas in Central Honshu, Nara, and Mie produce Sencha, Bancha, and Kabusicha.

KYŌTO

Nagoya

Tōkyō

Yokohama

SHIZUOKA

Ōsaka

Okayama

Hiroshima

SHIZUOKA PREFECTURE

Located on the Pacific side of the main island of Honshu, Shizuoka is responsible for half of Japan's tea output and produces mostly Sencha tea. The region experiences wet, cool weather, which is ideal for var. *sinensis*.

Shikoku
Kōchi

Fukuoka

Kumamoto

agasaki

Kyushu

KAGOSHIMA

East China Sea

KEY

⅄ **NOTABLE TEA-PRODUCING REGIONS**

▨ **AREA OF PRODUCTION**

ARACHA

Japan is famous for its green teas, which go through a unique production process. After plucking, the tea leaves are partially processed (steamed, rolled, and dried) into a crude tea called "Aracha". This is purchased by tea brokers and then "finished" into various teas, such as Sencha, by master sorters.

KAGOSHIMA PREFECTURE

Located on Kyushu, the southernmost island of Japan, Kagoshima has 15 tea-growing regions and is famous for a wide selection of styles of green tea – Gyokuro, Sencha, Bancha, and Kamairicha. Other producing areas of Kyushu are Saga, Fukuoka, and Miyazaki.

JAPANESE CHANOYU

Chanoyu, which translates as "hot water for tea", is a meditative ritual. Also known as Chado, or "Way of Tea", it is believed that through performing the ritual motions of tea preparation, it is possible to reach enlightenment.

The purpose of the Chanoyu ceremony is to prepare a simple and pure cup of powdered green tea (Matcha), through prescribed movements using specific teaware and implements. There are two types of tea ceremony. The first, Chakai, which is shown here, is an informal tea meeting that lasts under an hour. Usicha (thin Matcha) is served with Wagashi (sweets) to cut through the bitterness of

the tea. The second, Chaji, is a very formal ceremony lasting four hours, in which Koicha (thick Matcha) is prepared and served alongside an elaborate four-course meal, or "kaiseki".

Originally a Zen Buddhist ceremony, Chanoyu was refined by tea master, Sen no Rikyu in the 16th century. He outlined the principles of harmony, respect, purity, and tranquility. His tea ceremony practices are still taught around the world.

CHASEN
Carved from a single piece of bamboo, this tea whisk has multiple tines that are curled at the ends.

KENSUI
After the chawan has been rinsed, water is poured in to the kensui, or waste bowl, which is supposed to go unnoticed during the ceremony.

CHAWAN
There are different shaped tea bowls for different seasons – shallow for summer and deep for winter. They are made by hand and have a simple and humble aesthetic known as "wabi".

CHAKIN
White cloth used ritually to clean the tea bowl.

FUTA-OKI
When the lid from the tetsubin (kettle) is removed, it is placed on this lid rest, which is made of bamboo.

HISHAKU
A long bamboo ladle used to scoop hot water from the kettle.

MIZUSASHI

This vessel is used for holding fresh water to be heated in the tetsubin (kettle). It may be made of wood, a rough ceramic, or porcelain.

CHASHAKU

Often made of bamboo, this long thin spoon is used to scoop Matcha from the natsume (tea caddy) in to the chawan (tea bowl).

NATSUME

The natsume is used to hold Usucha (thin matcha powder) and can be made of lacquered or unlacquered wood.

KAMA

An iron kettle used to heat water taken from the mizusashi.

WAGASHI

Japanese sweets, called wagashi, made of rice flour, sugar, and adzuki bean paste are presented to guests just before the tea is served. Guests bring kaishi (square pieces of paper) and a pick used to eat the sweets.

PERFORMING CHANOYU

Each stage of the Japanese tea ceremony is slow and purposeful. The presentation area is kept pure and clean at all times. Lids are replaced on vessels and cloths are refolded. Here is an introduction to some of the simpler steps in this revered ritual.

1 **To begin, the fukusa, a square silk cloth** used to clean and purify the tools used in the ceremony, is folded. The fukusa is held by the two diagonal corners and a fold is made a third of the way down from the long edge.

2 **It is then folded down in the opposite** direction into thirds, folded in half lengthways, and, finally, in half again.

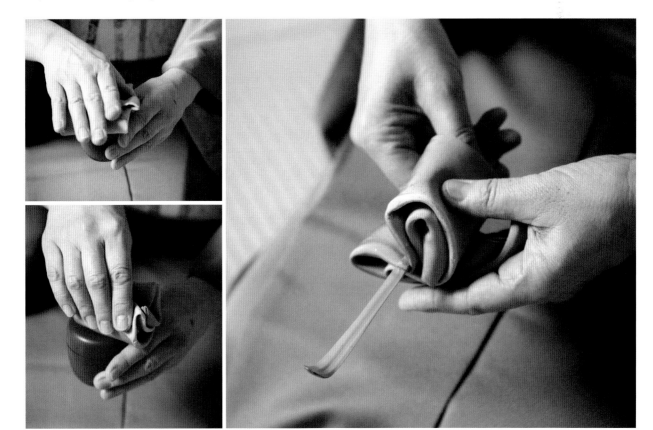

3 **The two edges are then folded into one another,** or over the implement to be purified. The host ritually cleans all of the implements in front of the guests in preparation for the ceremony.

4 **Hot water is collected** from the kama (kettle) using the ladle and poured into the chawan (bowl).

5 **The chasen (whisk) is inspected by the host** to make sure that it has no broken tines or worn areas, then placed in the chawan and rotated slowly. The water is whisked briefly and the whisk is removed. This softens, wets, and warms the whisk to keep it from staining.

6 **Warm water is rolled around** the chawan and then poured into the kensui. The chawan is then dried using the chakin.

7 **Two scoops of Matcha are placed** in the chawan using the chashaku.

8 **For a second time, the hishaku** is used to ladle water from the kama into the chawan, this time to make the Matcha tea. The hishaku rests on the kama when not in use.

9 **Tea is whisked slowly at first** and then briskly in a W pattern until froth forms on the surface of the tea.

10 **The host puts the bowl in her palm** and rotates the bowl twice in a clockwise direction, ending with the most ornate side of the chawan facing the guest.

11 **While still kneeling,** the host presents the tea to the guest, then bows.

THE ROLE OF THE GUEST
The guest bows to the host and turns the bowl twice clockwise so that the most favourable side of the chawan is now facing the host.

The guest consumes the tea in three sips. The last sip can be slurped to show the host that the guest enjoyed the good quality of the tea.

The guest gives the empty chawan back to the host.

RUSSIAN TEA CULTURE

Traditionally brewed using water heated in a samovar, tea has been enjoyed in Russia since the 17th century, when it was brought to the country from China. Today, tea is so popular in Russia that it is considered the national beverage.

Tea was first introduced to Russia in 1638, when it was gifted to Tsar Mikhail I by the Mongolians. A few decades later, the Russians sampled tea from China, and in 1679, signed a treaty with the Chinese for a regular supply of tea in exchange for animal furs.

By the 1870s, both loose black and brick tea were being imported from China, and tea had become inextricably linked with the Russian way of life. Marriages were arranged, business deals sealed, and differences resolved over a cup of tea.

Tea was prepared using water heated in a self-heating boiler called a samovar. A dense tea concentrate, or "zavarka", which had a tea-to-water ratio of 5 teaspoons of loose black tea per cup, was brewed in a teapot, or "chainik". The chainik was placed on top of the samovar to warm.

The lady of the house would pour the zavarka into glass cups and add additional hot water from the samovar, diluting the strength to suit the guest's taste. Tea was usually taken black, or with lemon, and sweetened with jam, honey, or sugar. It was accompanied by snacks, such as "syrniki", which are thick cheese pancakes served with jam, and small biscuits known as Russian tea cakes, made with ground nuts, butter, and flour, and rolled in icing sugar. Traditionally, the hot tea glasses were placed in metal holders, or "podstakannik", which allowed the drinker to sip the hot tea without burning their fingers.

In modern Russia, tea is still served at most social occasions, with loose tea being far more popular than the tea bag. Although the traditional samovar is now rarely used in everyday life, it remains a powerful symbol of Russian society, invoking positive feelings of warmth, comfort, and togetherness.

SAMOVAR
Originally utilitarian in design, samovars came to be highly decorative pieces of art.

Although "podstakannik" are no longer commonly used in Russian homes, they are still used to serve tea on trains.

TAIWAN

With a short but remarkable history of tea, the island of Taiwan is best known for the fragrant, fine-quality oolong teas, such as Tie Guan Yin and Ali Shan, that form the bulk of its production.

Taiwan, or Formosa as it was formerly known, was occupied by the Chinese in 1683, during the rule of the Qing dynasty, and became part of the Fujian province of China. Resettlers from the Wuyi mountains in Fujian brought their tea-growing skills with them and planted seeds on Taiwan's fertile mountains. As there were no manufacturing facilities in Taiwan, the tea was sent to Fujian for processing.

In 1868, British trader John Dodd helped to set up a plant in Taipei to process tea. This made manufacturing and exporting tea easier, giving Formosa tea worldwide recognition. Though

famous for its high-grown mountain oolongs, Taiwan is also known for producing many different styles of oolong, which are shipped worldwide and widely enjoyed in Taiwan.

The flavours of Taiwanese oolongs change seasonally. High mountain oolongs harvested in spring have a pronounced floral and fruity flavour, while oolongs harvested in the cooler winter weather are full-bodied with a fragrant aroma. The production methods for oxidized oolongs are quite time-consuming, the majority taking more than two days and up to 10 stages of production to complete.

HARVESTING TEA
Hand-picking is the preferred method for harvesting premium leaves in Taiwan, which are picked mainly as buds and young leaves.

TAIWAN KEY FACTS

PERCENTAGE OF WORLD PRODUCTION: 0.6%

MAIN TYPES: OOLONG, BLACK, GREEN

FAMOUS FOR: HIGH MOUNTAIN OOLONGS

HARVEST: 5 TIMES A YEAR FROM APRIL–DECEMBER

ELEVATION: MEDIUM–HIGH

80 PER CENT OF THE TEA GROWN IN TAIWAN IS BOUGHT BY ITS TEA-LOVING DOMESTIC MARKET

ASIA

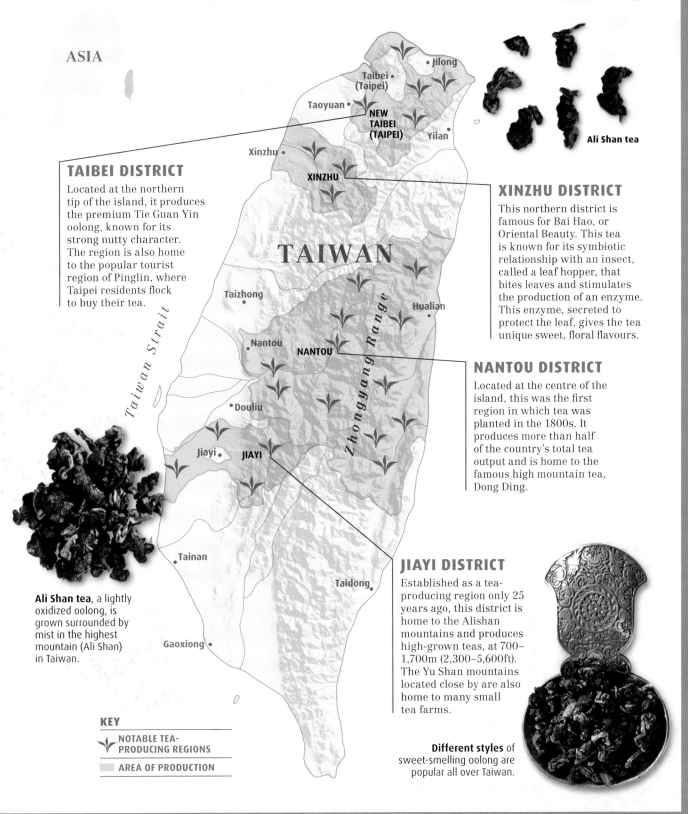

Ali Shan tea

TAIBEI DISTRICT

Located at the northern tip of the island, it produces the premium Tie Guan Yin oolong, known for its strong nutty character. The region is also home to the popular tourist region of Pinglin, where Taipei residents flock to buy their tea.

XINZHU DISTRICT

This northern district is famous for Bai Hao, or Oriental Beauty. This tea is known for its symbiotic relationship with an insect, called a leaf hopper, that bites leaves and stimulates the production of an enzyme. This enzyme, secreted to protect the leaf, gives the tea unique sweet, floral flavours.

NANTOU DISTRICT

Located at the centre of the island, this was the first region in which tea was planted in the 1800s. It produces more than half of the country's total tea output and is home to the famous high mountain tea, Dong Ding.

Ali Shan tea, a lightly oxidized oolong, is grown surrounded by mist in the highest mountain (Ali Shan) in Taiwan.

JIAYI DISTRICT

Established as a tea-producing region only 25 years ago, this district is home to the Alishan mountains and produces high-grown teas, at 700–1,700m (2,300–5,600ft). The Yu Shan mountains located close by are also home to many small tea farms.

Different styles of sweet-smelling oolong are popular all over Taiwan.

KEY

NOTABLE TEA-PRODUCING REGIONS

AREA OF PRODUCTION

TEA CUPS FROM AROUND THE WORLD

Tea drinking cups are available in many different shapes, sizes, and materials. Influenced by various cultural requirements and stylistic trends, they are an important part of the tea-drinking experience.

JAPANESE CHAWAN

Meaning "tea bowl" in Japanese, the chawan is a clay vessel often glazed with unusual designs. During the Japanese tea ceremony, or "Chanoyu" (see pp98–103), the host ensures that the most pleasing side of the bowl faces the guest.

TIBETAN TEA BOWL

Po Cha, the Tibetan butter tea, is served in this style of bowl. The wide mouth allows for grains, which are often added to the tea, to be scooped out easily.

RUSSIAN TEA GLASS AND HOLDER

In Russia, tea is traditionally served in a glass cup placed inside a filigreed metal holder, or "podstakannik". The holder protects the hands from the heat of the glass and improves the stability of the cup.

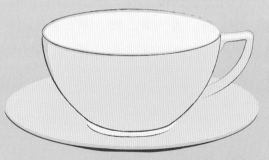

PORCELAIN CUP AND SAUCER

The cup and saucer is the universally recognized symbol for tea in the West. During the 16th and 17th centuries, porcelain cups and saucers were shipped from China to the West (hence the name "china"). Manufacturing began in England and other parts of Europe only in the mid-1700s, when a Jesuit priest living in China sent the recipe for the porcelain method to France.

TURKISH TEA GLASS AND SAUCER

Holding the top of this tulip-shaped glass with its outward curving mouth protects the drinker's hands from the heat. The glass also shows off the tea's rich amber hues.

INDIAN KULLARH

These simple, disposable handmade clay cups are ubiquitous at roadside tea stalls in India. More intricate, stylized versions are available in upmarket shops, too – a meeting of tradition and modernity.

CHINESE TEA CUP

Tea cups in China are small, which encourages light sipping when tasting high-quality teas. Usually made of porcelain, the cups are sometimes glazed with earthen colours or traditional blue and white patterns.

MOROCCAN TEA GLASS

Used for Moroccan mint tea, these decorative glasses, or "keesan", are available in a range of designs and colours.

TEA MUG

Popular throughout the UK and USA and available in a range of materials, such as porcelain, ironstone, and earthenware, mugs usually hold a large volume of tea, reducing the need for multiple refills.

SOUTH KOREA

Very little of South Korea's tender and delicious teas are exported, but it is worth seeking them out. Tea tourists arrive in Korea every year for the festivals that celebrate the delicate new spring teas.

Tea seeds were brought to Korea from China in 828CE and planted on Mount Jiri in South Gyeongsang province, giving birth to a thriving tea culture. In the 16th century, however, when Japan invaded the country, many tea fields were lost. In these and later periods of political turmoil, monks and scholars continued to grow tea in small areas, keeping the tea culture alive. It was only in the early 1960s that interest in tea revived, and tea fields were replanted.

Almost all of South Korea's tea is grown in the mountainous southern part of the peninsula where it enjoys sea breezes from the Korea Strait and the East Sea.

Most of the tea produced is green tea, picked according to the lunar calendar. Ujeon, made from the earliest pick in mid-April has sweet, soft flavours. Sejak is plucked in early May and has soft but more pronounced flavours. Jungjak is the latest harvest, in mid- to end of May, which gives the liquor a bright jade colour and very sweet flavours. Some artisans also produce an aged black tea called Balhyocha, which has flavours of malt, stone fruit, and pine.

BOSEONG
Verdant rows of tea plants in Boseong, a popular tea destination for tourists and considered Korea's tea-growing capital.

SOUTH KOREA KEY FACTS

PERCENTAGE OF WORLD PRODUCTION: 0.1%

FAMOUS FOR: SPRING TEA FESTIVALS

ELEVATION: MEDIUM

MAIN TYPES: GREEN, MATCHA, AGED BLACK

HARVEST: MID-APRIL–END MAY

Dried Korean tea in bamboo baskets waiting to be sorted and packaged.

ASIA

SOUTH GYEONGSANG PROVINCE

Green tea is produced from the tea plants growing on the slopes of Jiri San mountain. After the leaves are harvested they are "fixed" in woks at high temperatures to prevent oxidation. After heating, they become pliable and are rolled on rice mats into twisted shapes and are then dried in rotating driers. Farms in this area produce around 600 metric tonnes per annum.

SOUTH JEOLLA PROVINCE

This area is not quite as mountainous as South Geongsang and has tea gardens that attract tourists all year. Over 1,000 small tea farms covering 1,063 hectares (2,627 acres) flourish in the Boseong area. Many of the farmers are artisan tea makers. The famous Daehan Dawon tea fields are a major draw for Koreans. A working tea farm, it is open year-round and overlooks landscapes of rolling tea hills.

JEJU

This small island supports 84 tea farms, occupying an area of 341 hectares (843 acres). Most of the tea produced on Jeju Island is consumed by South Koreans, but about 90 metric tonnes is exported to North America.

KOREAN GREEN TEAS ARE PAN-FIRED TO PREVENT OXIDATION

KEY

NOTABLE TEA-PRODUCING REGIONS

AREA OF PRODUCTION

KOREAN DARYE

A simple yet formal tea ceremony, Korean Darye takes its cues from Zen Buddhism to celebrate and savour the simple things in life. This philosophy is reflected in the clean lines and natural feel of the teaware.

The modern approach to the Korean tea ceremony has been greatly influenced by the book *The Korean Way of Tea* (1973) in which Korean tea master Hyo-dang described the best way to prepare tea, especially Panyaro green tea, which is used in the Korean ceremony. The word "Panyaro" translates to "dew of enlightening wisdom", indicating the spiritual benefits that are derived from the preparation of this type of tea. Hyo-dang also founded the Korean Association for the Way of Tea, with the aim of preserving the traditional Korean methods of preparing and enjoying locally grown tea.

"DARYE" TRANSLATES TO "ETIQUETTE FOR TEA"

The Darye ceremony is closely connected to Zen Buddhism and its values of simplicity, and Koreans have embraced it as a way of slowing down and relaxing the mind in everday life.

The simplicity of the ceramic teaware adds to the aesthetic of the ceremony. Teaware is usually plain and muted in colour, and functional in form.

TONGS
These wooden tongs are used to scoop tea leaves from the tea container into the teapot.

WOODEN COASTERS
These are used to hold the tea cups while serving guests.

TEA CLOTH
This small cotton cloth is folded into a square and used for holding tea cups and other teaware.

WASTE WATER BOWL
This large ceramic bowl is used to collect waste water emptied from tea cups.

LINEN CLOTH
This is laid on the table under the teaware.

STAND FOR TEAPOT LID
The teapot lid rests on this ceramic stand when water or tea leaves are being placed in the tagwan.

COOLING BOWL
The small groove on the rim of this medium-sized ceramic bowl allows for easy pouring.

TAGWAN
A ceramic teapot, usually with a hollow side handle.

TEA CONTAINER
This ceramic container with a lid is used to hold the green tea.

CERAMIC CUPS
In summer, the ceremony calls for the use of "katade", wide, shallow bowls that cool the hot water; while taller "irabo" cups, used in winter, are designed to retain heat.

PERFORMING DARYE

The Korean Darye ceremony is marked by simplicity. The precise yet graceful movements of the host preparing the tea is a visual delight.

1 **Hot water is poured from a kettle** into the cooling bowl. Holding the bowl with both hands, and using the tea cloth to catch any drips, the host pours the water into the teapot.

2 **The water is poured from the teapot** into the cups, starting with the cup for the guest. This is to warm the teaware while the tea is being prepared.

3 **Hot water is again poured** from the kettle into the cooling bowl, then the teapot lid is removed.

4 **The tea container is opened (see inset)** and 4 pinches of tea leaves are taken out with the tongs and placed in the teapot.

5 **Using both hands, the host pours water** from the cooling bowl into the teapot. The lid is replaced (see inset) and the tea is left to steep for 2–3 minutes.

6 **The water in the cups** is emptied into the waste water bowl.

7 **The host pours** a small amount of tea to taste to ensure that the tea is ready for the guests to drink.

8 **The host pours the tea** into the cup that is the furthest away from her and works back to her own cup, filling the cups only half full and pausing for a few seconds between each cup.

9 **The host continues to pour**, this time starting from her own cup to the furthest guest's until the cups are three-quarters full. This is to ensure fair distribution of tea, and an even infusion.

10 **The guest's cup** is placed on a wooden saucer before it is served.

11 **The tea is placed** on the serving table in front of the guest.

THE ROLE OF THE GUEST

The tea cup is held with both hands around the middle of the body. Then it is lifted to the mouth and taken in three sips. The first sip is taken to enjoy the colour of the tea; the second sip for the aroma; and the third sip for the taste.

TURKEY

Turkey's climate is well suited to growing tea and the nation has developed quite a thirst for the beverage. The average person drinks up to 10 cups of tea per day of "Çay", the traditional black tea served strong and sweet.

EUROPE

Tea is grown in the picturesque province of Rize in northeast Turkey, an area located between the Pontic mountains and the Black Sea. Characterized by high temperatures and evenly distributed rainfall throughout the year, the humid, subtropical climate of this region is ideal for growing tea. In addition, cooler nights make it possible to grow tea without the use of pesticides.

The Rize province is quite rural and was an economically poor area before tea was first planted there in the 1940s. Since then tea production has spread along the local coastline of the Black Sea. The tea industry in Turkey now produces almost as much tea as Sri Lanka and has made a significant contribution to the local economy. Only 5 per cent of Turkish-grown tea is exported and the government imposes a 145 per cent import tariff on tea imports, ensuring that domestic consumption remains high.

Turkey is one of the few countries outside Italy to grow bergamot citrus, a principal ingredient in Earl Grey tea.

TURKEY KEY FACTS

PERCENTAGE OF WORLD PRODUCTION:

4.6%

MAIN TYPES:

BLACK (CTC)

HARVEST:

MAY–OCTOBER

FAMOUS FOR:

HIGH DOMESTIC CONSUMPTION

TEA GROWN WITHOUT PESTICIDES

ELEVATION:

MEDIUM

KEY

⅄ NOTABLE TEA-PRODUCING REGIONS

▬ AREA OF PRODUCTION

TEA IS OFFERED IN TURKISH BAZAARS TO ENGAGE CUSTOMERS AND SEAL DEALS

RIZE PROVINCE

On the sloping hills edging the Black Sea, tea is harvested using hand clippers, which slice the leaf rather than pluck it. The leaf is destined for CTC production (see p21). Harvesting starts early in the morning and ends in early evening. Most of the day's harvest is sold to one of several government factories.

ENJOYING TURKISH TEA

Turkish tea is prepared as a strong infusion of black tea in "çaydanlık", a set of two teapots, one resting on the other. The lower teapot is used to boil water, while the upper one keeps the concentrated infusion warm. This infusion is poured into tulip-shaped glasses, and water from the lower teapot is used to dilute the tea to the desired strength. Traditionally, Turkish tea is served black, without milk, and is taken with a number of sugar cubes.

Turkish black tea is served either "koyu", strong and dark, or "açik", weak and light.

VIETNAM

Vietnam's monsoon climate creates the perfect natural conditions for growing tea. Harvests are abundant, making Vietnam the sixth largest tea producer in the world.

The indigenous wild tea tree, or "shan", has been growing in Vietnam for at least 1,000 years. However, it was only in the 1820s that tea plantations were established by French immigrants. Production experienced a setback during the troubled years following World War II, but has since seen a strong recovery. Some regional specialty teas, such as Ha Giang and Shan Tuyet green tea and lotus blossom tea, are grown in the northern area of Vietnam. These teas are being promoted by the Vietnam Tea Association (VITAS) at tea markets worldwide to help farmers increase their income. Producers mostly use the orthodox (whole leaf) method of tea production, as well as some CTC (see p21).

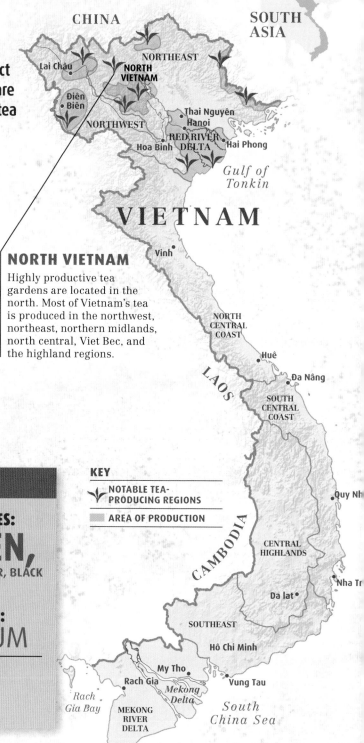

NORTH VIETNAM

Highly productive tea gardens are located in the north. Most of Vietnam's tea is produced in the northwest, northeast, northern midlands, north central, Viet Bec, and the highland regions.

KEY

↳ NOTABLE TEA-PRODUCING REGIONS

▨ AREA OF PRODUCTION

VIETNAM KEY FACTS

PERCENTAGE OF WORLD PRODUCTION: 4.8%

MAIN TYPES: GREEN, LOTUS FLOWER, BLACK

FAMOUS FOR: INDIGENOUS PLANTS

ELEVATION: MEDIUM

HARVEST: MARCH–OCTOBER

NEPAL

The cold mountain air and rugged terrain of Nepal are ideal for producing full-flavoured, complex teas. While black tea is most widely cultivated, green, white, and oolong teas are also produced.

ASIA

Tea production is relatively new to Nepal, where there are around 85 plantations and several small farms. Most of the farmers are smallholders who sell their leaves to central factories for processing.

Though large tea plantations mostly produce CTC

teas (see p21), some of the smaller farms produce excellent orthodox tea. Unlike black teas grown at lower elevations, Himalayan black teas do not fully oxidize because the high altitude at which they are processed causes the leaves to dry out during withering. The finished leaf will include flecks of green among the dark leaves and, although light in colour, the liquor will have the recognizable rich taste of black tea.

CHINA

INDIA

FAR WESTERN

Jumlā

MID WESTERN

Dipāyal

Birendranagar

Salyān

WESTERN

Pokharā

NEPAL

HIMALAYAS

CHINA

Kathmandu

CENTRAL

EASTERN

Dhankutā

Ilām

Birātnagar

INDIA

INDIA

Nepali black tea is grown in the eastern mountainous regions of the island.

NEPAL KEY FACTS

PERCENTAGE OF WORLD PRODUCTION: 0.4%

MAIN TYPES: BLACK GREEN, OOLONG

FAMOUS FOR: INNOVATING A YOUNG TEA INDUSTRY, USING **SMALL TEA FARM CO-OPERATIVES**

HARVEST: FIRST FLUSH **MARCH–APRIL** MONSOON FLUSH **JUNE–SEPTEMBER** AUTUMN FLUSH **OCTOBER**

ELEVATION: HIGH

DHANKUTA Dhankuta shares the same terroir as Ilam and neighbouring Darjeeling.

ILAM VALLEY Located at the eastern end of the country, bordering Darjeeling, this is the largest tea-growing area in Nepal.

KEY

 NOTABLE TEA-PRODUCING REGIONS

AREA OF PRODUCTION

KENYA

Tea was first introduced to Kenya in 1903, and its commercial production began in 1924. Since then, the Kenyan tea industry has become known for its black teas, demand for which has made the country the third largest producer in the world.

Tea in Kenya is grown at high altitudes, up to 2,700m (8,850ft), in the volcanic red soils of the highlands of the Rift Valley. Owing to their locations on the Equator, tea-growing regions of Kenya receive heavy rainfall and abundant sunshine, as well as cooler temperatures owing to the high elevation. These offer ideal conditions for growing tea, and allow for a year-long harvest.

Kenya grows *Camellia sinensis* var. *sinensis*, and produces about 5 per cent orthodox tea, with the rest entirely black CTC (see p21). Kenyan CTC is popular in classic breakfast teas, lending a familiar flavour associated with a round and full blend. Some larger granules of CTC tea are enjoyed as loose leaf tea rather than in tea bags.

Tea is mainly grown in the highlands on either side of the Great Rift Valley, namely the Kericho, Nandi, Nyeri, and Muranga regions, on farms of 0.40 hectare (1 acre) or less. The Kenya Tea Development Agency (KTDA) has been responsible for the success of small farms participation in the industry.

HARVESTING
Almost 90 per cent of Kenya's tea is hand picked and produced using the orthodox method.

KENYA KEY FACTS

PERCENTAGE OF WORLD MARKET: **7.9%**

MAIN TYPE: **BLACK, GREEN, WHITE**

HARVEST: JANUARY–DECEMBER

ELEVATION: HIGH

FAMOUS FOR: LARGE, HIGH-YIELD PRODUCTION AREAS

Marinyn, a spicy and full-bodied black tea is grown in the Kenyan highlands between Mount Kenya and Lake Victoria.

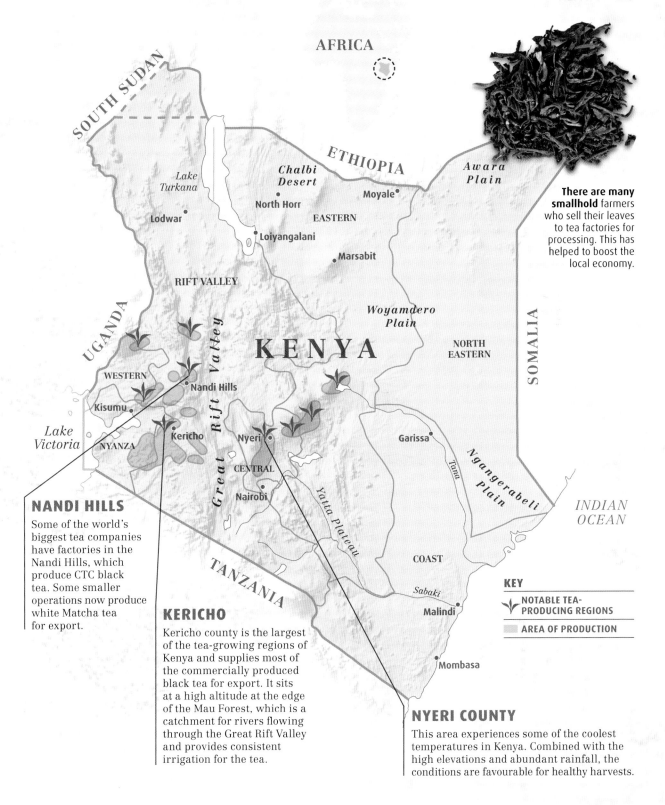

AFRICA

SOUTH SUDAN

ETHIOPIA

Lake Turkana

Chalbi Desert

Awara Plain

Moyale

North Horr

Lodwar

EASTERN

Loiyangalani

Marsabit

RIFT VALLEY

There are many smallhold farmers who sell their leaves to tea factories for processing. This has helped to boost the local economy.

Woyamdero Plain

UGANDA

KENYA

NORTH EASTERN

SOMALIA

WESTERN

Nandi Hills

Kisumu

Lake Victoria

NYANZA

Kericho

Nyeri

Garissa

Ngangerabeli Plain

CENTRAL

Nairobi

Tana

INDIAN OCEAN

NANDI HILLS

Some of the world's biggest tea companies have factories in the Nandi Hills, which produce CTC black tea. Some smaller operations now produce white Matcha tea for export.

Great Rift Valley

Yatta Plateau

COAST

TANZANIA

KERICHO

Kericho county is the largest of the tea-growing regions of Kenya and supplies most of the commercially produced black tea for export. It sits at a high altitude at the edge of the Mau Forest, which is a catchment for rivers flowing through the Great Rift Valley and provides consistent irrigation for the tea.

Sabaki

Malindi

Mombasa

KEY

⚘ NOTABLE TEA-PRODUCING REGIONS

▨ AREA OF PRODUCTION

NYERI COUNTY

This area experiences some of the coolest temperatures in Kenya. Combined with the high elevations and abundant rainfall, the conditions are favourable for healthy harvests.

INDONESIA

With a tropical climate and volcanic soil, Indonesia is conducive to tea cultivation, producing an average of 142,400 metric tonnes per year. It is best known for its dark and rich black teas.

The Dutch first planted var. *sinensis* seeds in Indonesia in 1684. However, this variety failed to flourish, and in the mid-1800s, they found that var. *assamica* was more suited to Indonesia's tropical climate. In the late 19th century, the first batch of black tea was shipped to Europe. Tea production thrived for several decades, but declined during World War II, when the Japanese occupied

the islands. The tea gardens fell into disrepair and did not recover, but in the late 1980s, a revitalization programme initiated by the government helped to revive tea production. Tea now accounts for 17 per cent of Indonesia's agricultural output. Although Indonesia produces some good oolongs and greens, it has always been best known for its full-bodied black teas.

NORTH SUMATRA

There are some tea gardens in North Sumatra that use the CTC method (see p21) to produce commercial tea, which is exported for the blending and tea bag industries.

JAVA

The best tea, manufactured using the orthodox method of production, is grown on the island of Java at an altitude of 700–1,500m (2,500–5,000ft). There are several plantations and small gardens in East Java, Banten, and near Bogor.

KEY

⌄ NOTABLE TEA-PRODUCING REGIONS

▬ AREA OF PRODUCTION

INDONESIA KEY FACTS

PERCENTAGE OF WORLD PRODUCTION: 3.2% | **ELEVATION:** HIGH

HARVEST: YEAR ROUND, BUT SOME OF THE BEST TEAS ARE PICKED IN

JULY–SEPTEMBER

MAIN TYPES: BLACK, OOLONG, GREEN

THAILAND

Although tea production is concentrated in a small area of the northern province, Thailand consistently produces excellent quality oolong, green, and black teas.

Bringing var. *sinensis* cuttings from Taiwan, the Chinese began to cultivate tea in Thailand in the 1960s. Thailand has since introduced new cultivars from Taiwanese cuttings suited to its cooler mountainous terroir. Tea is now grown in the northern provinces of Chiang Rai and Chiang Mei, in the Doi Mae Salong region in particular. Thai oolongs are produced in a similar way to Taiwanese rolled oolongs and typically have a medium level of oxidation. They are often described as having fragrant and grassy flavours with a creamy and nutty finish.

DOI MAE SALONG

Located near the Burmese border, this region is the centre of tea production and has elevations over 1,200m (4,000ft). Oolong, green, and black teas are grown in this region.

SOUTHEAST ASIA

THAILAND KEY FACTS

GLOBAL TEA PRODUCTION:

1.7%

MAIN TYPES:

OOLONG,
GREEN, BLACK

FAMOUS FOR: FRAGRANT OOLONGS, PARTNERSHIP WITH **TAIWAN** FOR **RESEARCH** AND **DEVELOPMENT**

HARVEST:
MARCH–OCTOBER

ELEVATION:

MEDIUM

KEY

↙ NOTABLE TEA-PRODUCING REGIONS

▨ AREA OF PRODUCTION

MOROCCAN TEA CULTURE

The custom of drinking sweet green tea infused with mint originated in Morocco in the 19th century, when Gunpowder tea was introduced by British merchants. In just 150 years, tea drinking has become an intrinsic part of Moroccan culture.

Moroccan mint tea, also known as Maghrebi tea, is popular in the Maghreb region of Tunisia, Algeria, and Morocco. It is prepared using Gunpowder green tea, which was first imported to Morocco in the 1860s. The Moroccans soon found that, when mixed with mint and sugar, it made a refreshing, aromatic drink.

In northern Africa, tea is always the first order of business, and it is customary to make tea for guests in honour of their visit. Unlike Maghrebi food, which is usually prepared by women, tea is brewed and served by the man of the house. It is considered impolite to refuse an offer of tea.

The host begins by rinsing two tablespoons of Gunpowder tea leaves in a teapot with boiling water. This reduces the bitterness of the tea. Next, he adds up to 12 cubes of sugar to the teapot and infuses the leaves with 800ml (1¾ pints) of boiling water for 15 minutes. This produces a very strong tea, which helps to explain why so much sugar is used. The tea is strained into a second metal teapot and brought to the boil before the sugar is added. When the tea is ready, handfuls of fresh mint leaves are placed in the traditional jewel-coloured glasses known as "keesan". Finally, the tea is poured with a flourish from a height of about 60cm (24in) to aerate the tea and create froth.

Traditionally, tea is served three times, imparting a different flavour each time as the leaves continue to steep. As an old proverb says, "The first glass is gentle as life; the second glass is as strong as love; the third glass is as bitter as death".

THE SWEETNESS OF THE SUGAR AND FRESH PIQUANCY OF THE MINT BALANCE THE ROBUST FLAVOUR OF THE TEA

Moroccan mint tea is prepared in "breds", metal teapots that can be heated on coal, and served in "keesan", traditional tea glasses found in most Moroccan households.

UNITED STATES OF AMERICA

Due to geographically varied tea-growing zones and climatic contrasts, tea cultivation has been a challenge for the US. However, new investment in tea farms throughout the country is boosting tea production.

In the 1880s, the US government began to experiment with tea growing in the states of Georgia and South Carolina. These farms failed within the first few decades owing to climate problems or the high cost of production. Since then, a number of farms around the country have been planting tea with positive results. One in particular, the Charleston Tea Plantation in South Carolina, is well established and provides the official tea of the White House. The soil conditions and temperature ranges across the country make it difficult to plan

for consistent harvests, so farmers are experimenting with various cultivars of tea plants to see which will thrive in their climate. Most of the 900 acres (364 hectares) of tea plantations in the US are planted in coastal states to benefit from the cooling ocean breeze. Farms in South Carolina, Alabama, California, Oregon, Washington, and Hawaii, have had productive harvests and have begun to sell their tea. Newer farms in Mississippi have thriving plants, and are set to harvest the leaves in a few years.

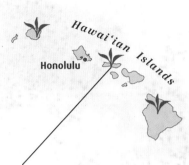

HAWAII

There are 50 small tea farms occupying 20 hectares (50 acres) around the islands of Hawaii, most of them located on "Big Island". The rich volcanic soil, mountainous terrain, and abundant rainfall are well-suited to the artisanal white, green, black, and oolong teas produced. Hawaiian tea is among the highest priced in the world. A Hawaiian tea farm has sold its tea to Harrods for £6,500 per kilo.

US KEY FACTS

PERCENTAGE OF WORLD PRODUCTION: 0.009%

MAIN TYPES: BLACK, GREEN, OOLONG

FAMOUS FOR: TEA FARM START-UPS WITH GARDENS RANGING IN SIZE FROM 1–81 HECTARES (1–200 ACRES)

HARVEST: APRIL–OCTOBER

ELEVATION: LOW–HIGH

COOL TEMPERATURES
This Mississippi tea farm is attempting to cultivate plants that will adjust to cold temperatures. These young cuttings will be ready to harvest in 3-4 years.

NORTH AMERICA

WASHINGTON AND OREGON

Tea in these states is grown in gardens of 5 acres (2 hectares) and produced as artisanal tea. Green, white, and oolong teas are produced.

TEA IS GROWN ON 900 ACRES OF LAND IN THE COASTAL STATES

Seattle
WASHINGTON

CANADA

ROCKY MOUNTAINS

MONTANA

NORTH DAKOTA

MINNESOTA

MAINE

OREGON

IDAHO

WYOMING

SOUTH DAKOTA

Minneapolis

WISCONSIN

MICHIGAN

VT
NH

NEW YORK

MA
CT RI

NEBRASKA

IOWA

Chicago

OHIO

New York

PENNSYLVANIA NEW JERSEY

Francisco

NEVADA

UNITED STATES

ILLINOIS

INDIANA

Washington DC

DE
MD

CIFIC
EAN

UTAH

COLORADO

OF AMERICA

KANSAS

Missouri

WEST VIRGINIA

VIRGINIA

CALIFORNIA

KENTUCKY

Ohio

APPALACHIAN MOUNTAINS

NORTH CAROLINA

Los Angeles

ARIZONA

NEW MEXICO

OKLAHOMA

Arkansas ARKANSAS

MISSOURI

TENNESSEE

Mississippi

SOUTH CAROLINA

MEXICO

TEXAS

LOUISIANA

MISSISSIPPI

ALABAMA

GEORGIA

ATLANTIC OCEAN

Austin

New Orleans

FLORIDA

Gulf of Mexico

The tea plants grown are mostly natural hybrids of var. *assamica* and var. *sinensis*.

KEY

⌄ NOTABLE TEA-PRODUCING REGIONS

▨ AREA OF PRODUCTION

MISSISSIPPI

In 2014, The Great Mississippi Tea Company, with the assistance of Mississippi State University, planted 289 acres (117 hectares) with over 30,000 tea plants, with more being added each year. Collecting and testing hybrids, as well as integrated pest control, are being monitored in this new enterprise.

WADMALAW ISLAND, SOUTH CAROLINA

With a sub-tropical climate and 1,320mm (52in) annual rainfall, the island is ideal for tea production. Its 52 hectares (127 acres) are harvested by machines and black tea is processed at the on-site factory using the orthodox method.

TISANES

WHAT IS A TISANE?

Consumed for their therapeutic properties, as well as their relaxing and rejuvenating aromas, tisanes are infusions of aromatic herbs and plants. Served either hot or cold, they are a delicious alternative to caffeinated beverages.

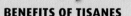

TEA OR TISANE?

Contrary to popular belief, not all hot herbal beverages can be categorized as tea. Tisanes are often wrongly referred to as "herbal teas", but as they are not made from the *Camellia sinensis* plant they are not tea in the strict sense. Instead, tisanes use all parts of various other plants – bark, stems, roots, flowers, seeds, fruit, and leaves – to make an infusion. With the exception of yerba mate, tisanes do not contain caffeine.

BENEFITS OF TISANES
Containing aromatherapeutic properties, tisanes soothe and rejuvenate both body and mind.

HEALING POWERS OF TISANES

For centuries, healing tisanes have been used in traditional Chinese medicine and Indian Ayurvedic medicine to treat the symptoms of various health problems. With the growing popularity of tisanes in the West, wellness blends and mixtures that help to detox, calm and relax, induce sleep, or treat cold and flu symptoms are now widely available in tea shops and supermarkets. In fact, there is probably a blend or infusion available for almost every kind of ailment.

Plants and herbs have a complicated chemistry and may not mix well with conventional medicines, or may aggravate allergies. Always check with your healthcare professional before deciding to make tisanes a part of your healing plan.

THE HERBALIST

Nicholas Culpeper (1616–1654) was an English physician, apothecary, astrologist, and botanist. His *Complete Herbal* book, a compendium of hundreds of tisane ingredients and their medicinal properties, has been used as a reference since it was published. Every known tisane ingredient at the time is detailed with specific instructions to treat ailments. Practising as a physician in Spitalfields, London, he combined his knowledge of astrology and apothecary to treat his patients. He was considered a radical in his day.

HOME REMEDY
With their natural healing properties, tisanes are easy home remedies for common ailments.

A combination of lavender, hibiscus, and rosehip packs a powerful punch of vitamin C and can help treat colds.

ROOTS

As the lifeline of a plant, roots draw nutrients from the soil and carry them to the leaves and flowers. Thick and fibrous in texture, they contain potent organic compounds that make them an excellent ingredient for herbal tisanes.

Roots have their own micro-culture of organisms, insects, and nutrients, which gives them health-giving properties. If growing in temperate areas, the roots absorb nutrients from the soil and store them during winter, when the plant's metabolism slows down. They are best harvested on a dry day in spring, just as the plant comes to life. Roots can either be hung to dry, provided they are not too thick or soft, or dried slowly in a dehydrator. Pre-dried roots are widely available to buy as well.

ROASTED DRIED ROOTS CAN BE USED AS CAFFEINE-FREE TEA SUBSTITUTES

BURDOCK ROOT
(Arctium)
Part of the same plant that produces burrs – the prickly seed pods that stick to clothing when brushed against – the tap root of the burdock plant can grow up to 60cm (24in) in length. It contains inulin, a compound that supports probiotic health in the colon. Burdock root has been used to treat acne and joint pain, and is a good diuretic and blood-purifying agent. It is often used in detox tisanes as it helps cleanse the liver.

LIQUORICE
(Glycyrrhiza glabra)
This fibrous root imparts sweetness to a tisane. It can improve respiratory health by soothing inflamed mucous membranes of the throat and lungs, providing relief from colds; it similarly helps with ailments of the stomach and intestine. Liquorice is also used as a detoxifier and mood-enhancing tonic.

CHICORY
(*Cichorium intybus*)
The root of this wild plant, identified by its pretty blue flowers, is often used in tisanes. Like burdock root (see opposite), chicory contains inulin, which makes it a powerful probiotic agent. Chicory detoxifies, helps to strengthen the immune system, and is used to treat arthritis because of its anti-inflammatory qualities. It also has a sedative quality and is often used in tisanes to aid sleep.

DANDELION ROOT
(*Taraxacum officinale*)
Often considered an invasive weed, dandelion is frequently used in tisane mixtures owing to its anti-inflammatory qualities and ability to help reduce pain and swelling. It also aids digestion and supports good bacteria in the intestines.

GINGER
(*Zingiber officinale*)
Widely used as a culinary spice, ginger has become a popular ingredient in herbal infusions. It is an anti-inflammatory and helps detoxify the body; it contains terpene and ginger oil, which help stimulate blood circulation and cleanse the lymphatic system. Root ginger, therefore, is used to help treat digestive ailments, nausea, and the symptoms of colds and flu.

BARK

Like the roots, bark carries nourishing properties to the plant. Although bark is not the most commonly used part of a shrub or tree, it is becoming a popular tisane ingredient, with each type of bark imparting unique flavours and health benefits to the infusion.

The inner layers of the bark are a tree's powerhouse, nourishing and sustaining it, while the innermost rings of the trunk give the tree structural support. Improperly harvesting bark will permanently damage the tree, so foraging for it on your own is not advised; it is best to purchase bark that has been harvested from farmed trees. Whether you intend to consume the bark on its own or with other herbs, you need to prepare it as a decoction (see p145). When using bark with other herbs, infuse the dry herbs in boiling water for at least five minutes before adding the bark decoction.

WILD CHERRY
(*Prunus avium*)
Wild cherry, or choke cherry, bark has a soothing effect on coughs and is therefore used in many commercial cough medicines. It also contains prunasin, which helps to reduce inflammation caused by infection. It has an astringent, sometimes bitter taste, and is best blended with more pleasant-tasting herbs or fruits.

CINNAMON
(*Cinnamomum verum*)
Cinnamon bark's antioxidant properties are used to treat cold and flu symptoms, while its antibacterial properties aid digestion by reducing gas and stimulating appetite. This spice should be taken sparingly as it contains coumarin, a naturally occurring sweet compound that can damage the liver if taken in large doses. There are two varieties of cinnamon: Cassia and Ceylon. Grown in Sri Lanka, Ceylon cinnamon is considered to be superior as it contains less coumarin, making it a better choice for tisanes.

WILLOW BARK
(*Salix alba*)

One of the oldest herbs used to treat pain, willow bark contains salicin, which helps to relieve pain when it converts to salicylic acid in the body. Salicylic acid is used to make aspirin, which is a conventional pain reliever. A willow bark tisane is good for relieving cold and flu symptoms, headache, pain, and fever as it has anti-inflammatory properties.

BARKS ARE GREAT "COLD BUSTERS" AS THEY ARE SOOTHING, PAIN RELIEVING, AND HAVE ANTI-OXIDANT PROPERTIES

SLIPPERY ELM
(*Ulmus fulva*)

The mucilaginous (viscous) inner bark of the slippery elm has a soothing effect. It coats the tissues of the mouth, throat, stomach, and intestines, relaxing them and reducing inflammation.

FLOWERS

Fresh or dried flowers and petals are often used in tisanes because they add colour and flavour to the mix. Many also have anti-inflammatory and detoxifying properties, so contribute much more than just visual appeal to the drink.

CHAMOMILE

(*Matricaria chamomilla*)
A low-lying, daisy-like flower, chamomile will flourish even in gravel, or grow through cracks in the pavement. Used to treat insomnia and anxiety because of its mild sedative qualities, chamomile is an immune booster as well as a relaxant. Chamomile's pleasing pineapple aroma contributes to its calming effect.

Chamomile

ELDERFLOWER

(*Sambucus nigra*)
These white umbrella-shaped flower clusters grow on the elder shrub and bloom during the month of May. Known for their anti-inflammatory properties, the flowers are dried and used in infusions to detox the body and fight cold and flu symptoms. Sweet and fragrant, it makes a tasty addition to tisanes.

HIBISCUS

(*Hibiscus sabdariffa*)
Hibiscus is a common ingredient in herbal tisanes because it adds a deep red colour and a tart flavour. It contains anthocyanin, an organic compound that adds pigment to red and purple-coloured fruits and vegetables. Studies suggest that hibiscus may help to treat high blood pressure and maintain healthy levels of cholesterol. Hibiscus flowers also contain quercetin, an anti-inflammatory, which is good for digestive health and relieving the symptoms of arthritis.

LAVENDER
(*Lavandula angustifolia or Lavandula officinalis*)
Lavender is known for its distinct and relaxing aroma. When combined with lemon balm in a hot tisane it helps to relieve headaches. Lavender is a classic remedy for insomnia, fever, anxiety, stress, cold and flu symptoms, and digestive problems.

Lavender

RED CLOVER
(*Trifolium pratense*)
Red clover has a nectar-like sweetness. Its water-soluble chemicals, called isoflavones, have oestrogen-like qualities that may help reduce symptoms experienced by menopausal women. It is also known to lower bad cholesterol (LDL) and increase good cholesterol (HDL), thereby helping to improve heart health.

LIME FLOWER
(*Tilla vulgaris*)
Lime flower is the blossom of the linden tree; it is also known as linden flower. It contains antihistamine, often used to treat allergic reactions, and quercetin, a powerful antioxidant that neutralizes DNA-damaging free radicals and that also has anti-inflammatory properties. Linden flowers have been used in alternative medicine to treat coughs, and cold and flu symptoms. They are fragrant, and impart sweet, floral flavours to tisanes.

LEAVES

Herbal leaves contain a potent combination of sugars, proteins, and enzymes, all of which are beneficial to health. They also release flavours and aromas that range from calming to invigorating. This may explain the variety of leaves used in herbal tisanes.

LEMON BALM
(*Melissa officinalis*)
As the name suggests, this herb from the mint family has a lemony aroma and taste. It is used as a calming agent to ease anxiety and restlessness, and to treat the symptoms of cold and flu.

LEMON VERBENA
(*Aloysia triphylla*)
Also known as vervain, lemon verbena has potent lemon-like fragrant oils and may help to relieve fever and cold symptoms, calm nerves, and aid digestion.

MINT
(*Lamiaceae*)
Mint leaves (including peppermint and spearmint) have been used for hundreds of years to alleviate headaches and aid digestion. Do not use if you suffer from gastro-oesophageal reflux, as it could make the condition worse.

MULBERRY LEAF
(*Morus nigra*)
Often used in Japanese tisanes, the mulberry leaf tastes surprisingly sweet, and can help relieve a number of ailments such as coughs and cold and flu symptoms, fever, sore throat, and headache.

ROOIBOS
(*Aspalathus linearis*)
Also known as redbush, this oxidized herbal drink is mostly consumed as a caffeine-free black tea substitute and is also available as an unoxidized leaf. It provides a neutral base that blends well with fruits, spices, and other flavours. Rooibos contains antioxidants and helps with insomnia, digestion, and blood circulation. It grows only in the Western Cape region of South Africa.

TULSI
(*Ocimum tenuiflorum*)
Native to India, tulsi (or holy basil) has strong antioxidant properties, a sweet flavour, and fragrant aroma. It has been used to relieve headache, cold and flu symptoms, as well as anxiety, and boosts concentration and memory. The tulsi plant can absorb toxic chromium from the soil, so try to purchase it from an organic source.

BASIL
(*Ocimum basilicum*)
Basil is much more than a kitchen staple; it is a powerful anti-inflammatory, high in antioxidants, and helps treat the symptoms of cold and flu. The combination of sweet liquorice and savoury flavours makes it an interesting ingredient in herbal blends.

YERBA MATE
(*Ilex paraguariensis*)
Grown mostly in Brazil and Argentina, this evergreen plant is high in caffeine. It has faint hints of tobacco and green tea flavours, and is known to improve mental energy as well as mood.

GOURD AND BOMBILLA
Yerba mate is traditionally infused in a hollow gourd and sipped through a "bombilla", or straw.

FRUIT AND SEEDS

Full of vitamins and minerals with potent health-boosting properties, fruit and seeds not only enhance the healing effect of the tisane, but also improve the taste.

BLUEBERRIES

(Generally *Vaccinium cyanococcus*, and specifically *Vaccinium angustifolium*, wild blueberry) The dark bluish-purple colour of blueberries indicates the presence of anthocyanins – antioxidants that contribute to cell and cardiovascular health, and have cognitive benefits. Blueberries also contain the carotenoid lutein, which is associated with good eye health.

Blueberries

ELDERBERRIES

(*Sambucus nigra*) These dark indigo berries are from the same tree that produces the elderflower (see p138). They contain anthocyanins, which have strong antioxidant qualities, as well as the immune-boosting quercetin. Traditionally, elderberry has been used to treat coughs and colds. It is also good for eye and heart health. Only pick the dark purple, fully ripe berries, and avoid green or partially ripe berries and stems, as these are toxic. Elderberries may be dried, or dehydrated, for use in tisanes.

CITRUS PEEL

Either dried or freshly grated citrus peel can be used in tisanes. It acts primarily on the digestive and respiratory systems, and provides relief for sore throats, flu, and arthritis. Choose organic, unwaxed, pesticide-free citrus, as any harmful chemicals tend to remain on, and even in, the skin.

ROSEHIPS
(Rosa canina)
Found in hedgerows in most parts of the world, the best rosehips come from the wild rose, but many other effective varieties are available. Most health food stores and tea shops stock them. Rosehips contain very high amounts of vitamin C, antioxidants, and carotenoids, and are known to relieve the symptoms of cold and flu, headaches, and indigestion. They also provide nourishment to the skin because of their high antioxidant and bioflavonoid content. Their anti-inflammatory properties can help relieve arthritic swelling.

CARDAMOM
(Elettaria cardamomum)
Native to southeast Asia, the leaves of the cardamom plant can grow up to 3m (10ft) tall. Its seed pods contain small black seeds that should be crushed before adding to tisanes. Cardamom aids digestion and helps treat the symptoms of colds and flu. It also acts as a natural diuretic and antioxidant, and has detoxifying and anti-inflammatory benefits.

FENNEL
(Foeniculum vulgare)
Fennel, with its liquorice flavour, primarily aids digestion, and so is suitable as an after-dinner tisane. The seeds contain quercetin, the flavonoid antioxidant that has immune-boosting benefits. The anti-inflammatory properties of quercetin can help to relieve symptoms of arthritis.

Fennel

PREPARING TISANES

Part of the appeal of a tisane lies in its preparation. Making your own tisanes at home can be a rewarding experience, especially as you become familiar with the various ingredients, and how to dry and store them.

FINDING INGREDIENTS

You will easily be able to find all the herbs, spices, or fruits that you would like to use in your tisanes in health-food shops or online, but you can also grow many herbs, such as rosemary, mint, sage, and thyme, in your own garden. Other ingredients, such as ginger, cloves, and cinnamon, are everyday storecupboard items.

Exercise caution if you decide to forage for ingredients – avoid gathering anything from roadsides, where plants are exposed to exhaust fumes and your own safety may be at risk, or from places where chemical fertilizers and pesticides have been used. If gathering roots, ensure that you do not damage other plants nearby. Also, never use flowers from a florist for tisanes as they are usually heavily sprayed with insecticides.

Ready-made tisanes are widely available, too. Tea shops usually have a selection of tisanes with various flavours and aromas to cater to specific moods, and most supermarkets stock a range of tisanes, including immune-boosting blends to help fight colds.

ANTI-INFLAMMATORY
The combination of ginger, turmeric, and lemon is an anti-inflammatory and can help to relieve joint pain.

SAGE
A tisane made from sage can aid relaxation and is thought to ease anxiety and depression.

HOME-GROWN
Chamomile and lemon balm is a popular combination that calms the body and lifts the spirits. They are both easy to grow.

DRIED INGREDIENTS HAVE CONCENTRATED OILS THAT RELEASE THEIR GOODNESS IN HOT WATER

AIR-DRYING
Herbs, such as mint, are best air-dried indoors as this will help them retain their flavour and colour. A warm, dry spot is ideal for this.

DRYING AND STORING

If using foraged ingredients, wash them immediately under cold running water, then lightly pat them dry with a kitchen towel. Lay out the plants or herbs on a baking sheet, or place them in a basket and leave them to dry, covered with a light cloth or clean kitchen towel, in a warm, dry place. This may take several days, depending on the level of humidity. You can also dry them in an oven on a very low heat or in a dehydrator. Do not dry them in a microwave oven as it may cause scorching, and the rapid heating could damage some of the aromatic oils in the plants.

To store herbs – whether picked and dried or shop-bought – keep them in an airtight container made of glass, ceramics, or stainless steel, away from heat and other competing odours.

PREPARING INGREDIENTS

Fruits are best used fresh in tisanes. While plants may be used fresh, they will not be as potent in taste or aroma as when dried. This is because drying concentrates the oils and other components, which are released more easily when they are reconstituted in hot water. If infusing fresh herbs, use three times as much as dry.

To prepare your tisane, break the dried herbs into smaller pieces and measure 1 teaspoon of each herb per cup. Tisanes should be infused with freshly boiled water and steeped for approximately 5 minutes. Unlike tea, tisanes do not require different timings per type. As herbs are not oxidized, or processed in any way apart from drying, they do not require delicate treatment.

DECOCTIONS

Roots and stems need to be boiled in water to release their flavours and nutrients, a process known as "decoction". Boil the ingredients for 5–10 minutes, then strain and cool the liquid before drinking.

Use only stainless steel or glass pots to boil herbs. Do not use aluminium, iron, or copper cookware, as the chemical composition will affect the essence and integrity of the ingredients.

WELLNESS TISANES

Tisanes can be thought of as all-round wellness tonics, infusions that soothe and heal with their medicinal properties. With aromas that engage the sense of smell and evoke positive emotions, they can even help you heal and rejuvenate before you've taken a sip. The overall effect of aroma and infusion calms both body and mind.

Here are some traditional uses for tisanes containing ingredients such as chamomile, lavender, lemon verbena, and mint. But before trying out a tisane, check with your healthcare provider, as some herbs may interfere with conventional medications, or increase the symptoms of allergies. If you are pregnant or breastfeeding, check with your doctor before experimenting with herbal tisanes.

DETOX

Tisanes that help to detox the body are made with herbs that cleanse the liver and expel unwanted chemicals and heavy metals, such as lead, cadmium, and mercury, from the body. This process is sometimes referred to as "chelating". Ingredients that chelate have the ability to bind to heavy metals and eliminate them from the body through the gastrointestinal tract. Classic detox blends include ginger, dandelion, burdock, and liquorice roots.

BEAUTY

Tisanes for skin, nail, and hair health are often called "beauty blends", and contribute to improved blood circulation and skin elasticity. Rose petals have an invigorating effect on the skin, and also help with the circulation. Bamboo leaf contains vegetative silica, which is believed to improve skin, hair, and nail health, while chamomile, lime flower, and lemon verbena leaf are said to improve the overall health and condition of the skin.

COLDS

So-called cold-busting tisanes are packed with antioxidants and Vitamin C. Some soothe the throat, while others are "cooling" to help regulate cold symptoms, such as fever. You might expect a powerful, medicinal-tasting mixture, but fragrant ingredients, such as elderflower, liquorice, cinnamon, ginger, rosehips, rosemary, and lemon verbena, each contribute in their own way to help relieve the symptoms of the common cold.

DRINKING DETOX TISANES CAN HELP TO CLEANSE THE SYSTEM

CALM

Tisanes that have a calming effect are primarily aromatic. This is because fragrances play a big part in the treatment of stress, anxiety, and insomnia. Some of these tisanes are mildly sedative, while others have an overall soothing quality. Classic ingredients in these restful blends include chamomile, lavender, lemon verbena, and basil.

DIGESTION

Ginger, liquorice root, wild cherry bark, cinnamon, hibiscus, cardamom, and fennel are all beneficial for digestive health. Tisanes blended to help with digestion often have a smooth texture and a soothing effect. They can be taken at any time, but are best consumed as an after-dinner beverage.

JOINTS

Ingredients with anti-inflammatory properties are helpful in treating arthritis and other joint problems. The flavonoid quercetin is found in dark-coloured fruits, such as cranberries and blueberries. Ginger and turmeric roots also possess anti-inflammatory properties and have shown signs of helping to relieve the symptoms of arthritis and joint pain.

THE ANCIENT EGYPTIANS USED TISANES FOR THEIR HEALING PROPERTIES

ROSEHIPS
A rosehip infusion will help fight the common cold. Add a spoonful of honey to mellow the tart flavour.

LAVENDER
Drinking a tisane containing lavender before bed can help aid a restful sleep.

CHAMOMILE
Immune-boosting chamomile pairs well with citrus fruits, such as lemon, for a light and refreshing infusion.

WHEEL OF WELLNESS

Plants have a number of medicinal properties and can be used to help treat various ailments. Use this wheel, which lists ingredients according to the medical conditions they can ease, as a guide to help you prepare your tisane.

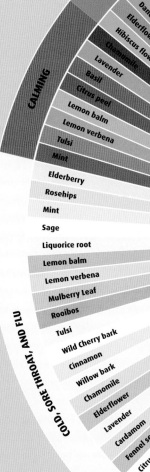

ARTHRITIS

Liquorice root
Linden flower
Citrus peel
Rosehips
Bamboo leaf
Basil
Wild Cherry bark
Willow bark
Cardamom
Fennel seed
Burdock root
Chicory root
Dandelion root
Elderflower
Hibiscus flower
Chamomile
Lavender
Basil
Citrus peel
Lemon balm
Lemon verbena
Tulsi
Mint

CALMING

Elderberry
Rosehips
Mint
Sage
Liquorice root
Lemon balm
Lemon verbena
Mulberry Leaf
Rooibos
Tulsi
Wild Cherry bark
Cinnamon
Willow bark
Chamomile
Elderflower
Lavender
Cardamom
Fennel seed
Citrus peel
Linden flower
Ginger

COLD, SORE THROAT, AND FLU

Dandelion root
Thyme
Linden flower
Liquorice
Slippery Elm
Ginger
Elderberry
Mulberry leaf
Burdock root
Dandelion root

COUGH

HIBISCUS AND ROSEHIPS

Hibiscus helps with high blood pressure and maintaining healthy levels of cholesterol. Rosehips are good for relieving the symptoms of cold and flu, as they contain high quantities of vitamin C, antioxidants, and carotenoids.

BURDOCK AND DANDELION ROOT

Burdock helps purify blood and is used to treat joint pain. Dandelion contains anti-inflammatory properties, reduces pain and swelling, and is used to detox.

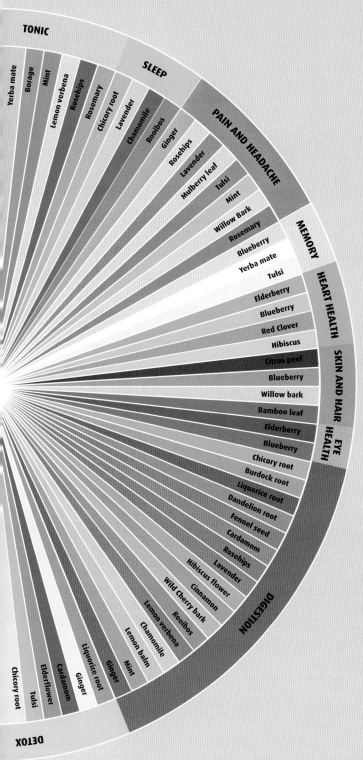

TONIC

Yerba mate
Borage
Mint
Lemon verbena
Rosehips
Rosemary
Chicory root
Lavender

SLEEP

Chamomile
Rooibos
Ginger
Rosehips
Lavender
Mulberry leaf
Tulsi
Mint

PAIN AND HEADACHE

Willow Bark
Rosemary
Blueberry
Yerba mate
Tulsi
Elderberry
Blueberry
Red Clover
Hibiscus
Citrus peel
Blueberry
Willow bark
Bamboo leaf
Elderberry
Blueberry

MEMORY

HEART HEALTH

SKIN AND HAIR

EYE HEALTH

Chicory root
Burdock root
Liquorice root
Dandelion root
Fennel seed
Cardamom
Rosehips
Lavender
Hibiscus flower
Cinnamon
Wild Cherry bark
Lemon verbena
Rooibos
Chamomile
Lemon balm
Mint
Ginger
Liquorice root
Cardamom
Elderflower
Tulsi
Chicory root

DIGESTION

DETOX

ROOIBOS

An infusion using rooibos helps treat insomnia, promote good digestion, and relieve the symptoms of cold and flu.

CHAMOMILE AND LAVENDER

Both chamomile and lavender are known for their fragrant aromas, which contribute to a sense of wellbeing. For this reason, both are often used in calming tisanes.

THE RECIPES

CITRUS JASMINE SERVES 4

 TEMP **80°C (175°F)**    INFUSE **3–4 MINS**   TYPE **HOT**   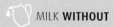 MILK **WITHOUT**

Jasmine tea is traditionally made at night as the flowers open. Green tea and jasmine flowers are stirred together, then the flowers are removed, the tea is baked, and the process is repeated over several evenings. Finger lime adds tanginess to this tea.

1 heaped tbsp **Jasmine Dragon Pearl tea leaves**

flesh of 1 **Australian finger lime**, or ½ **lime**, peeled and thinly sliced, plus extra slices, to garnish (optional)

900ml (1½ pints) **water** heated to 80°C (175°F)

1 tsp each of **lime**, **lemon**, and **orange zest**, to garnish (optional)

1 Place the tea leaves in a teapot and add the finger lime, reserving 1 tsp for garnishing.

2 Add the hot water and infuse for 3–4 minutes until the jasmine pearls start to open.

SERVE IT UP Serve hot, garnished with the reserved flesh of the finger lime or the lime slices, if using. Alternatively, garnish with the citrus zest.

DELICATE **FRESH** PERFUME

JADE ORCHARD SERVES 4

 TEMP **80°C (175°F)**   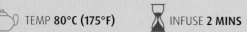 INFUSE **2 MINS**   TYPE **HOT**   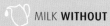 MILK **WITHOUT**

Green Snail tea has lovely roasted notes as a result of pan-firing over charcoal. Goji berries bring a slight tartness to the mix, but the pear balances the flavours with a bit of sweetness.

1 **pear**, cored and diced, plus 4 thin slices, to garnish

1 tbsp **dried goji berries**

200ml (7fl oz) boiling **water**, plus 750ml (1¼ pints) water heated to 80°C (175°F)

2 tbsp **Yunnan Green Snail tea leaves**

1 Place the pear and berries in a teapot, add the boiling water, and set aside to infuse.

2 Meanwhile, place the tea leaves in a separate teapot. Add the heated water and leave to infuse for 2 minutes.

3 Strain the tea into the fruit infusion.

SERVE IT UP Strain into cups and serve hot, garnished with a pear slice.

Jade Orchard A hot tea that is sweet, tart, and smoky all at once, this one is hard to put down.

LEMONY DRAGON WELL SERVES 4

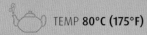 TEMP **80°C (175°F)**   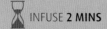 INFUSE **2 MINS**   TYPE **HOT**   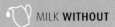 MILK **WITHOUT**

Use an everyday grade of Dragon Well for this recipe as the subtleties of a higher grade would be lost. Roasted walnuts bring out the wok-fired character of the tea, while lemon myrtle tones the roasted notes and sweetens the drink.

1¼ tsp **dried lemon myrtle**

1½ tsp **chopped roasted walnuts**

240ml (8fl oz) boiling **water,** plus 800ml (1⅓ pints) water heated to 80°C (175°F)

4 tbsp **Dragon Well tea leaves** (Long Jing)

1 Place the lemon myrtle and walnuts in a teapot. Add the boiling water and set aside to infuse.

2 Place the tea leaves in a separate teapot, add the heated water, and leave to infuse for 2 minutes.

3 Strain the tea into the fruit infusion.

SERVE IT UP Strain into cups and serve hot.

MOROCCAN MINT SERVES 4

 TEMP **90°C (195°F)**   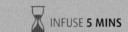 INFUSE **5 MINS**   TYPE **HOT**   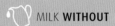 MILK **WITHOUT**

Strong and smoky in flavour after a long steep, Gunpowder tea is the key ingredient in Moroccan mint teas. Traditionally prepared by the man of the house, it has become the symbol of hospitality in Moroccan homes and shops.

4 tsp **Gunpowder tea leaves**

leaves from 6 large sprigs of **mint,** plus 4 sprigs, to garnish

900ml (1½ pints) **water** heated to 90°C (195°F)

5 tbsp **caster sugar**

1 Place the tea leaves and mint leaves in a teapot, add the hot water, and infuse for 5 minutes.

2 Strain the tea into a saucepan and add the sugar. Stir and bring to a simmer on a medium heat. Remove from the heat and pour the sweetened tea back into the teapot.

SERVE IT UP Pour into cups from a height of 30cm (12in) to create froth on the surface. Serve hot with a sprig of mint in each cup.

ROASTED
MINTY
SWEET

HONEY LEMON MATCHA SERVES 2

 TEMP **80°C (175°F)**    INFUSE **NONE**   TYPE **ICED**   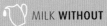 MILK **WITHOUT**

This iced Matcha tea is as green as chlorophyll. You can use a confectioner's grade of Matcha, which is not as expensive as the higher grades. The honey will add sweetness and the lemon juice will brighten the flavour.

5 tsp **honey**

1 tbsp **lemon juice,** plus some **lemon zest**

500ml (16fl oz) **water** heated to 80°C (175°F)

1½ tsp **Matcha powder**

ice cubes

1 Place the honey, lemon juice, zest, and half the hot water in a jug.

2 Put the Matcha powder in a bowl and add a little of the remaining hot water. Whisk the Matcha in a "W" motion to form a thin paste. Add the rest of the hot water and whisk until some froth begins to form on the surface.

SERVE IT UP Pour the Matcha mix into the jug, stir, and serve in tumblers filled with ice cubes.

CITRUS **SWEET** REVIVING

ICED SAVOURY SENCHA SERVES 2

 TEMP **80°C (175°F)**   INFUSE **1 MIN**   TYPE **ICED**   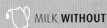 MILK **WITHOUT**

In this iced Sencha, thyme imparts a savoury note to the Japanese tea, whose name translates to "infused tea". Ginger provides some spice and gives a slight suggestion of sweetness.

2 tbsp **grated ginger**

4 sprigs of **thyme**

2 tbsp **Japanese Sencha tea leaves**

500ml (16fl oz) **water** heated to 80°C (175°F)

ice cubes

Special equipment

muddler, or pestle

1 Divide the ginger and thyme equally between 2 tumblers and muddle them, using a muddler or pestle.

2 Place the tea leaves in a teapot, add the hot water, and infuse for 1 minute.

3 Strain evenly into the tumblers. Cool, add the ice cubes, and serve.

TIP For a less diluted iced tea, make some Sencha infusion in advance and freeze in ice-cube trays, and use instead of normal ice cubes.

ICED DRAGON WELL SERVES 2

 TEMP **80°C (175°F)**   INFUSE **1 MIN**   TYPE **ICED**   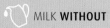 MILK **WITHOUT**

Rambutan, a spiky red and gold fruit from Asia, reveals a white lychee-like fruit under its thick skin. Although not as sweet as lychee, it is sweet enough to complement Dragon Well's pan-fired toasted and nutty flavours.

12 **rambutans**, fresh or canned, peeled and sliced

120ml (4fl oz) boiling **water**, plus 400ml (14fl oz) water heated to 80°C (175°F)

5 tbsp **Dragon Well tea leaves** (Long Jing)

ice cubes

Special equipment
muddler, or pestle

1 Set aside some pieces of rambutan for garnishing, and muddle the rest with a muddler or pestle.

2 Place the muddled fruit in a teapot and add the boiling water. Infuse for 4 minutes. Strain the infusion, cool, and pour into tumblers.

3 In a separate teapot, infuse the tea leaves in the heated water for 1 minute. Cool and pour into the tumblers.

SERVE IT UP Add the ice cubes and garnish with the reserved rambutan.

OSMANTHUS GREEN SERVES 2

 TEMP **80°C (175°F)**   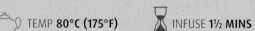 INFUSE **1½ MINS**   TYPE **ICED**   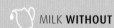 MILK **WITHOUT**

They may be small, but the yellow flowers of osmanthus are full of rich, sweet vanilla fragrance. They balance nicely with the vegetal notes of the tea, while the fruit adds a familiar sweetness.

1 **Asian water apple** or **pear**, cored and thinly sliced

250ml (9fl oz) boiling **water**, plus 250ml (9fl oz) water heated to 80°C (175°F)

2 tsp **Yunnan Green Snail tea leaves**

½ tsp dried **osmanthus flowers**

ice cubes

1 Set aside 2 apple slices for garnishing, place the remaining slices in a teapot, and add the boiling water. Leave to infuse.

2 Place the tea leaves and osmanthus flowers in a separate teapot. Add the heated water and infuse for 1½ minutes.

3 Strain into the fruit infusion and infuse for 3 minutes. Then strain into tumblers and allow to cool.

SERVE IT UP Add the ice cubes and garnish with the apple slices.

CREAMY SWEET PERFUME

MATCHA LATTÉ SERVES 2

 TEMP **80°C (175°F)**   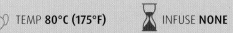 INFUSE **NONE**   TYPE **LATTÉ**    MILK **ALMOND**

There isn't a hint of bitterness in this blissfully creamy tea. The powdery Matcha makes a bubbly froth when whipped and imparts a pale green tinge to this easy-to-make choco-rich latté.

350ml (12fl oz) **plain sweetened almond milk**

15g (½oz) **white chocolate**

2 tsp **Matcha powder**, plus extra to garnish

120ml (4fl oz) **water** heated to 80°C (175°F)

Special equipment

electric hand whisk

1 Heat the milk and chocolate in a saucepan on a medium heat, stirring constantly, until the mixture simmers and becomes creamy. Remove from the heat and set aside.

2 Whisk the Matcha powder and hot water in a bowl to form a thin paste. Add the hot milk and chocolate mixture and whisk briskly until foamy. Pour into cups.

SERVE IT UP Garnish with a pinch of Matcha powder and serve hot.

VERBENA GREEN LATTÉ SERVES 2

 TEMP **80°C (175°F)**    INFUSE **1½ MINS**   TYPE **LATTÉ**   MILK **RICE**

Gunpowder tea leaves are a good choice for layering with other flavours. When the leaves are infused for a short time, they produce a light grassy flavour. A good low-fat latté option, the lemon flavour of verbena is sweet rather than tart.

350ml (12fl oz) **sweetened rice milk**

2 tsp **dried lemon verbena**

2 tbsp **Gunpowder tea leaves**

120ml (4fl oz) **water** heated to 80°C (175°F)

Special equipment

electric hand whisk

1 Heat the rice milk and lemon verbena in a saucepan on a medium heat until it starts to simmer. Remove from the heat and leave to steep for 4 minutes.

2 In a teapot, infuse the tea leaves in the hot water for 1½ minutes, then strain into a large bowl.

3 Strain the hot verbena rice milk mixture into the bowl and whisk together. Discard the leaves.

SERVE IT UP Pour into 2 cappuccino cups or mugs and serve hot.

GREEN HARMONY FRAPPÉ SERVES 2

 TEMP **80°C (175°F)**    INFUSE **4 MINS**   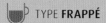 TYPE **FRAPPÉ**    MILK **ALMOND**

The citrussy notes of lemongrass brighten the vegetal and grassy flavours of Gunpowder tea. While the melon brings in sweetness, the almond milk creates a delightfully frothy frappé.

3 tsp **chopped fresh lemongrass**

2 tsp **Gunpowder tea leaves**

150ml (5fl oz) **water** heated to 80°C (175°F)

¼ **small honeydew melon**, diced, plus melon balls, to garnish

150ml (5fl oz) **sweetened almond milk**

ice cubes, crushed

Special equipment
blender

1 Place the lemongrass and tea leaves in a teapot. Add the hot water and infuse for 4 minutes.

2 Strain into a jug and set aside to cool to room temperature.

3 Place the melon in the blender and add the cooled tea and almond milk. Blend until creamy and frothy on the surface.

SERVE IT UP Pour into tumblers half-filled with crushed ice, and garnish with the melon balls.

COLD **CREAMY** FRESH

KOREAN MORNING DEW SERVES 2

 TEMP **80°C (175°F)**   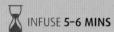 INFUSE **5-6 MINS**    TYPE **SMOOTHIE**    MILK **WITHOUT**

The leaves of Korean Junjak tea need to be infused for a bit longer than normal to give it strength. The blended result is a fragrant and unique flavour, reminiscent of Patbingsu, a Korean summer dessert of shaved ice and fruits.

2 tsp **Korean Junjak tea leaves**

175ml (6fl oz) **water** heated to 80°C (175°F)

240ml (8fl oz) **sweet aloe juice**

1 **pear**, cored and thinly sliced

ice cubes, finely crushed

Special equipment
blender

1 Place the tea leaves in a teapot, add the hot water, and infuse for 5-6 minutes.

2 Strain into a jug and set aside to cool to room temperature.

3 Pour the cooled tea and aloe juice into a blender. Set aside 2 pear slices and add the remaining to the blender, and blend until smooth and frothy.

SERVE IT UP Pour into tumblers half-filled with crushed ice and garnish with the reserved pear slices.

APRICOT REFRESHER SERVES 2

 TEMP **80°C (175°F)**    INFUSE **1 MIN**   TYPE **SMOOTHIE**   MILK **WITHOUT**

Mao Jian translates as "downy tip" because of the fine hairs that appear on this bud tea. It has a sweet vegetal flavour. Apricot gives the smoothie a beautiful colour and an extra sweetness.

2 tsp **Mao Jian tea leaves**

150ml (5fl oz) **water** heated to 80°C (175°F)

120ml (4fl oz) **plain yogurt**

5 **apricots**, fresh or canned, pitted and sliced

2 tbsp **honey**

Special equipment
blender

1 Place the tea leaves in a teapot, add the hot water, and leave to infuse for 1 minute.

2 Remove the tea leaves and allow the infusion to cool.

3 Place the yogurt, apricots, and honey in the blender. Add the cooled tea and blend until creamy.

SERVE IT UP Pour into tumblers and serve immediately.

COCONUT MATCHA SERVES 2

 TEMP **NONE**    INFUSE **NONE**   TYPE **SMOOTHIE**   MILK **COCONUT CREAM**

Naturally sweet and creamy, this smoothie is a great afternoon pick-me-up. The coconut cream brings healthy fatty acids to the mix, while the avocados provide a good dose of potassium and vitamins K and C.

8 tbsp **coconut flakes**

½ **avocado**

1 tsp **Matcha powder**

120ml (4fl oz) **chilled coconut cream**

240ml (8fl oz) **chilled coconut water**

Special equipment
blender

1 Preheat the oven to 180°C (350°F/ Gas 4). Place the coconut flakes on a baking tray and toast for 4½ minutes, or until golden brown.

2 Place the flakes in the blender along with the remaining ingredients and blend until creamy.

SERVE IT UP Serve in chilled glasses with a straw.

Little Green Snail This aromatic tea packs quite a punch with the combined flavours of rosemary and Soju.

LITTLE GREEN SNAIL <small>SERVES 2</small>

 TEMP **80°C (175°F)**    INFUSE **3½ MINS**   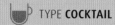 TYPE **COCKTAIL**    MILK **WITHOUT**

Soju is a distilled Korean rice liquor, which carries a bit of a kick. Look for a soju with 20 per cent alcohol; anything stronger may overpower the tea. Rosemary gives an aromatic lift to this well-balanced cocktail.

5 tsp **Yunnan Green Snail tea leaves**

300ml (10fl oz) **water** heated to 80°C (175°F)

½ tsp **roughly chopped rosemary**, plus 2 sprigs, to garnish

200ml (7fl oz) **soju** or **vodka**

ice cubes

Special equipment
cocktail shaker

1 Place the tea leaves in a teapot, add the hot water, and leave to infuse for 3½ minutes.

2 Add the chopped rosemary to the teapot and infuse for a further 30 seconds. Then strain into the cocktail shaker and leave to cool.

3 Add the soju and ice cubes to the cocktail shaker and shake for a few seconds.

SERVE IT UP Strain into cocktail glasses and garnish each with a sprig of rosemary.

JASMINE EVENING <small>SERVES 2</small>

 TEMP **80°C (175°F)**    INFUSE **3 MINS**    TYPE **COCKTAIL**    MILK **WITHOUT**

If you like floral flavours, you will probably love this fragrant and fruity cocktail. As the alcohol will absorb a lot of the tea flavour, this drink uses more tea than when simply enjoyed on its own.

3 tbsp **Jasmine Dragon Pearl tea leaves**

400ml (14fl oz) **water** heated to 80°C (175°F)

2 tsp **quince syrup**

90ml (3fl oz) **white rum**

ice cubes

Special equipment
cocktail shaker

1 Place the tea leaves in a teapot and add the hot water. Leave to infuse for 3 minutes.

2 Strain the infusion into the cocktail shaker, add the syrup, and leave to cool.

3 Add the rum and the ice cubes to the cocktail shaker and shake for a few seconds.

SERVE IT UP Strain into cocktail glasses and serve immediately.

ICED TEA SERVES 4

In the United States, tea is most often enjoyed sweet and cold. Ask for tea at a restaurant and be prepared to be served a tall glass of icy cold tea. Here is a simple recipe to make your own at home.

Iced tea is new to some parts of the world, but has been consumed in America for over a century. The invention of iced tea is attributed to Richard Blechynden, a tea company representative from England who was promoting Indian tea at the St. Louis World's Fair (Missouri, USA) in 1904. The weather was unbearably hot at the fair, and the small cups of hot tea he was offering for sampling were not generating much interest. So he added ice to the tea and it became a big hit.

There are two types of classic iced tea – sweet iced tea, popular in the Southern states, and unsweetened iced tea (without sugar), popular in the north. A lemon wedge is sometimes added to either. This version of iced tea is a favourite south of the Mason-Dixon line.

YOU WILL NEED

Ingredients

6 tsp loose black tea

500ml (16fl oz) boiling water

pinch of baking soda

175g (6oz) caster sugar

2 lemons, sliced, to serve (optional)

ice cubes

Cool teas were enjoyed in the Southern states as early as the 1830s and usually involved the addition of Champagne to a cooled green tea.

1 Place the tea leaves in a teapot and add the boiling water. Steep for 15 minutes to create a strong infusion.

2 Carefully pour the tea into a heatproof jug using a strainer.

80 PER CENT OF TEA CONSUMED IN THE UNITED STATES IS IN THE FORM OF ICED TEA

3 While the tea is still hot, add the baking soda (to prevent the tea from clouding) and sugar, and stir well until dissolved. Add 1.5 litres (2⅔ pints) cool water and stir to mix. Leave to cool until lukewarm, then transfer to the fridge and chill for 2–3 hours. Add the lemon slices to the chilled tea, if desired. Add enough ice cubes to fill the jug.

FRESHEN UP
The perfect pick-me-up on a warm sunny day, iced tea is best served in clear glasses that display its warm amber colour.

HAZELNUT PLUM DELIGHT SERVES 4

 TEMP **85°C (185°F)**   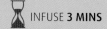 INFUSE **3 MINS**   TYPE **HOT**   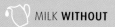 MILK **WITHOUT**

The woodland flavours of Longevity White provide a good foundation for this mellow blend. Toasted hazelnuts impart a sweet smokiness, while the dark-skinned plums lend a pink tinge.

4 tbsp **toasted hazelnuts**, crushed

4 **purple plums**, sliced

120ml (4fl oz) boiling **water**, plus 750ml (1¼ pints) water heated to 85°C (185°F)

7 tbsp **Longevity White tea leaves** (Shou Mei)

1 Place the hazelnuts and plums in a teapot. Add the boiling water and set aside to infuse.

2 Place the tea leaves in a separate teapot, add the heated water, and leave to infuse for 3 minutes.

3 Strain into the plum infusion and infuse for a further 1 minute.

SERVE IT UP Strain into cups and serve hot.

GOLDEN SUMMER SERVES 4

 TEMP **85°C (185°F)**   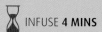 INFUSE **4 MINS**   TYPE **HOT**   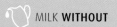 MILK **WITHOUT**

This drink derives its name from the golden liquor of tea and the amber colour of apricots. The fruit and almonds bring to the surface the sweet flavours found in White Peony tea, recalling summer orchards.

4 **apricots,** cut into wedges

3 drops **pure almond extract**

120ml (4fl oz) boiling **water**, plus 750ml (1¼ pints) water heated to 85°C (185°F)

6 tbsp **White Peony tea leaves** (Bai Mu Dan)

1 Place the apricots in a teapot with the almond extract. Add the boiling water and leave to infuse.

2 Place the tea leaves in a separate teapot, add the heated water, and infuse for 4 minutes.

3 Strain the tea into the apricot infusion and infuse for a further 2 minutes.

SERVE IT UP Strain into cups and serve hot.

ROSE GARDEN SERVES 4

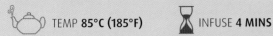 TEMP 85°C (185°F)   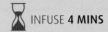 INFUSE 4 MINS   TYPE HOT   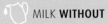 MILK WITHOUT

White Peony doesn't contain any flowers in spite of its name, but has lovely hints of forest and herbs. Cardamom highlights these flavours and lifts the fragrance of the rosebuds used.

20 **dried rosebuds,** plus 4 extra, to garnish

½ tsp **crushed cardamom seeds**

boiling **water,** to rinse, plus 750ml (1¼ pints) water heated to 85°C (185°F)

7 tbsp **White Peony tea leaves** (Bai Mu Dan)

honey, to taste (optional)

1 Rinse the rosebuds and cardamom seeds with boiling water and set aside.

2 Place the tea leaves in a teapot, add the heated water, and infuse for 4 minutes.

3 Strain the tea into a separate teapot. Add the rinsed rosebuds and cardamom seeds, and infuse for a further 3 minutes.

SERVE IT UP Strain into cups and add some honey, if desired. Serve, garnished with a rosebud.

NORTHERN FOREST SERVES 4

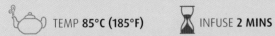 TEMP 85°C (185°F)   INFUSE 2 MINS   TYPE HOT   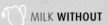 MILK WITHOUT

This white tea presents notes of pine, which become more pronounced as it cools. Sweet and resinous juniper berries are often found growing at the edge of a pine forest, so are a natural companion.

3 tbsp **toasted crushed pine nuts**

6 **fresh** or 12 **dried juniper berries,** crushed, plus extra, to garnish

120ml (4fl oz) boiling **water**, plus 750ml (1¼ pints) water heated to 85°C (185°F)

6 tbsp **Longevity White tea leaves** (Shou Mei)

1 Preheat the oven to 180°C (350°F/Gas 4). Place the pine nuts on a baking tray and toast for 3 minutes, or until golden brown.

2 Place the berries and pine nuts in a teapot and add the boiling water. Set aside to infuse.

3 Place the tea leaves in a separate teapot, add the heated water, and infuse for 2 minutes. Then strain the tea into the juniper infusion and infuse for a further 4 minutes.

SERVE IT UP Strain into cups and garnish with a few juniper berries.

WHITE PEONY PUNCH SERVES 2

 TEMP 85°C (185°F)   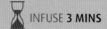 INFUSE 3 MINS   TYPE ICED   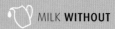 MILK WITHOUT

This tea version of May wine, a popular European white wine punch, uses green grapes to give a subtle hint of white wine. The addition of sweet woodruff imparts a pungent sweetness to the tea.

18 **seedless green grapes,** halved

2 tsp **dried sweet woodruff**

120ml (4fl oz) boiling **water**, plus 400ml (14fl oz) water heated to 85°C (185°F)

4 tbsp **White Peony tea leaves** (Bai Mu Dan)

ice cubes

Special equipment
muddler, or pestle

1 Place half the grapes in a teapot and muddle with a muddler or pestle. Add the remaining grapes and woodruff, and add the boiling water. Leave to cool.

2 Place the tea leaves in a separate teapot, add the heated water, and infuse for 3 minutes. Then strain into 2 tumblers and leave to cool.

SERVE IT UP Strain the fruit infusion into the tumblers and add the ice cubes.

REFRESHING SWEET PUNGENT

FIGS ON THE TERRACE SERVES 2

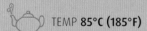 TEMP 85°C (185°F)   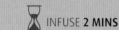 INFUSE 2 MINS   TYPE ICED   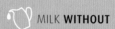 MILK WITHOUT

Sweet figs and aromatic sage combine in this summer tea that transports you to an Italian "cucina". Make sure you use the sage with care as it has quite a powerful flavour.

2 **fresh** or **dried figs**, quartered

2 **fresh sage leaves**, or ¼ tsp **dried whole sage leaves**

100ml (3½ fl oz) boiling **water**, plus 400ml (14fl oz) water heated to 85°C (185°F)

2 tbsp **Longevity White tea leaves** (Shou Mei)

ice cubes

Special equipment
muddler, or pestle

1 Divide the figs and sage equally between 2 tumblers and muddle with a muddler or pestle. Add the boiling water and leave to cool.

2 Meanwhile, place the tea leaves in a teapot, add the heated water, and infuse for 2 minutes. Then strain into the tumblers and stir to mix with the fig and sage infusion. Leave to cool.

SERVE IT UP Stir and add the ice cubes before serving.

Figs on the Terrace Sweet and refreshing, this iced tea is just right for a summer afternoon.

LYCHEE STRAWBERRY FRAPPÉ SERVES 2

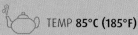 TEMP **85°C (185°F)**   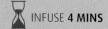 INFUSE **4 MINS**   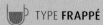 TYPE **FRAPPÉ**   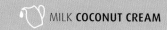 MILK **COCONUT CREAM**

A cooling summer drink, the sweet fruit helps to bring out the flavour of this tea. Make sure you infuse the tea for the full time, so that it has a strong flavour, and serve with coconut cream for added richness.

3 tbsp **Longevity White tea leaves** (Shou Mei)

240ml (8fl oz) **water** heated to 85°C (185°F)

8 **lychees**, from a can

8 **strawberries**

5 **ice cubes**

125ml (4½fl oz) **coconut cream,** whipped

Special equipment

blender

1 Place the tea leaves in a teapot, add the hot water, and infuse for 4 minutes. Strain and cool for a few minutes.

2 Pour the cooled tea into a blender, add the lychees and strawberries, and blend until smooth and frothy.

3 Add the ice cubes and blend again until the ice cubes are just crushed.

SERVE IT UP Pour into tumblers and serve topped with whipped coconut cream.

TANGLED GARDEN SERVES 2

 TEMP **90°C (195°F)**   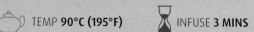 INFUSE **3 MINS**   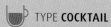 TYPE **COCKTAIL**   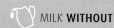 MILK **WITHOUT**

This cocktail brings together fragrant elderflower and the bold flavour of white tea. Mixed with vodka and served chilled, it makes for a truly unique drink with a slight kick.

6 tbsp **White Peony tea leaves** (Bai Mu Dan)

400ml (14fl oz) **water** heated to 90°C (195°F)

4 tsp **elderflower syrup**

120ml (4fl oz) **vodka**

ice cubes

Special equipment

cocktail shaker

1 Place the tea leaves in a teapot and pour over the hot water. Infuse for 3 minutes, then strain into a cocktail shaker and leave to cool completely.

2 Add the elderflower syrup and vodka to the cocktail shaker. Then add enough ice to fill the shaker. Shake briskly for 30 seconds to combine.

SERVE IT UP Strain into cocktail glasses and serve immediately.

FRAGRANT
SWEET
RICH

HIGH MOUNTAIN COMFORT SERVES 4

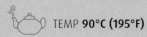 TEMP **90°C (195°F)**   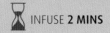 INFUSE **2 MINS**   TYPE **HOT**   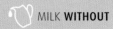 MILK **WITHOUT**

Mediterranean dried blackcurrants are suggested for this recipe as they have a distinct taste compared to those that grow in hedgerows. Their raisin-like sweetness works well with lightly oxidized oolong tea varieties.

4 tbsp **dried blackcurrants**

1½ tsp **crushed roasted almonds**

300ml (10fl oz) boiling **water**, plus 600ml (1 pint) water heated to 90°C (195°F)

2 tbsp **Taiwan High Mountain tea leaves**

1 Place the blackcurrants and almonds in a teapot and add the boiling water. Set aside to infuse.

2 Rinse the tea leaves with some of the heated water to help them open faster.

3 Place the tea leaves in a separate teapot and add the remaining heated water. Infuse for 2 minutes, then strain into the fruit infusion.

SERVE IT UP Strain into cups and serve hot.

ROASTED FRAGRANT SWEET

CHOCOLATE ROCK SERVES 4

 TEMP **85°C (185°F)**   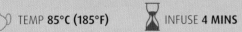 INFUSE **4 MINS**   TYPE **HOT**   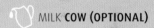 MILK **COW (OPTIONAL)**

Roasted walnuts, cacao nibs, and oolong come together to bring a warming campfire feel to this infusion. Add milk to help the roasted natural oils from the walnuts and cacao rise to the surface and enhance the flavour of the drink.

4 tbsp **crushed cacao nibs**, shells included

2 tbsp **crushed roasted walnuts**

300ml (10fl oz) boiling **water**, plus 600ml (1 pint) water heated to 85°C (185°F)

4 tbsp **Wuyi Rock tea leaves**

1 Place the cacao and walnuts in a teapot, add the boiling water, and leave to infuse.

2 Place the tea leaves in a separate teapot and add the heated water. Infuse for 4 minutes.

3 Strain the tea into the cacao and walnut infusion. Leave to infuse for a further minute.

SERVE IT UP Strain into cups, add milk if desired, and serve hot.

Rocking Cherry Earthy, spicy, and fruity notes highlight this Wuyi Rock oolong tea.

ROCKING CHERRY SERVES 4

 TEMP **85°C (185°F)**　　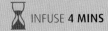 INFUSE **4 MINS**　　 TYPE **HOT**　　 MILK **WITHOUT**

Wuyi Rock oolong roasted leaves have an earthy depth and a slightly floral aroma. Cherries complement this tea's natural flavours and the nutmeg brings out the spice notes in the leaves.

12 **cherries**, pitted and halved

pinch of **ground nutmeg,** plus extra to garnish

300ml (10fl oz) boiling **water,** plus 600ml (1 pint) water heated to 85°C (185°F)

4 tbsp **Wuyi Rock tea leaves**

Special equipment
muddler, or pestle

1 Muddle the cherries in a teapot with a muddler or pestle. Then add the nutmeg and the boiling water and leave to infuse.

2 Place the tea leaves in a separate teapot, add the heated water, and infuse for 4 minutes.

3 Strain the tea into the fruit infusion.

SERVE IT UP Strain into cups and serve hot with a small sprinkling of nutmeg.

GRAPE GODDESS SERVES 4

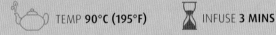 TEMP **90°C (195°F)**　　 INFUSE **3 MINS**　　 TYPE **HOT**　　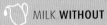 MILK **WITHOUT**

Green grapes lighten this infusion in taste and colour, and give it a fruity sweetness suggestive of a dry white wine. The fragrant tea anchors the infusion with deep, sweet flavours.

15 **seedless green grapes,** halved

150ml (5fl oz) boiling **water,** plus 750ml (1¼ pints) water heated to 90°C (195°F)

2 tbsp **Iron Goddess of Mercy tea leaves** (Tie Guan Yin)

Special equipment
muddler, or pestle

1 Place half the grapes in a teapot and muddle them gently with a muddler or pestle to release some juice. Add the remaining grapes, then add the boiling water and set aside to infuse.

2 Place the tea leaves in a separate teapot, add the heated water, and infuse for 3 minutes.

3 Strain the tea into the grape infusion and leave to infuse for a further 3 minutes.

SERVE IT UP Strain into cups and serve hot.

ICE GODDESS SERVES 2

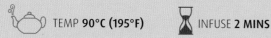 TEMP **90°C (195°F)**   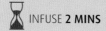 INFUSE **2 MINS**   TYPE **ICED**   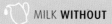 MILK **WITHOUT**

A lightly oxidized oolong, Iron Goddess has delicate floral notes and a subtle sweetness. While aromas of lemon zest work better than acidic lemon juice, Asian pear florals meld perfectly with the tea's perfumes.

2 tsp **lemon zest**

4 slices of **Asian pear**

1 heaped tbsp **Iron Goddess of Mercy tea leaves** (Tie Guan Yin)

500ml (16fl oz) **water** heated to 90°C (195°F)

ice cubes

2 thin **lemon slices**, to garnish

Special equipment

muddler, or pestle

1 Divide the lemon zest equally between 2 tumblers and muddle with a muddler or pestle. Place 2 pear slices in each tumbler.

2 Place the tea leaves in a teapot, add the hot water, and infuse for 2 minutes. Strain into a jug and leave to cool.

3 Pour the tea into the tumblers.

SERVE IT UP Add the ice cubes, stir, and garnish each with a slice of lemon.

CHILLED ROCK OOLONG SERVES 2

 TEMP **90°C (195°F)**   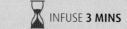 INFUSE **3 MINS**   TYPE **ICED**   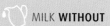 MILK **WITHOUT**

The mild toasty flavour of Wuyi Rock oolong tea balances the tanginess that comes from kumquat, a small oval-shaped citrus fruit that is sour on first bite, but surprisingly sweet thereafter.

2 **kumquats**, cut into 12 rounds, plus 2 slices, to garnish

1 tsp **ground nutmeg**

150ml (5fl oz) boiling **water**, plus 350ml (12fl oz) water heated to 90°C (195°F)

5 tbsp **Wuyi Rock tea leaves**

ice cubes

1 Place the kumquat slices and the nutmeg in a teapot and add the boiling water. Infuse for 3 minutes, then strain into 2 tumblers and leave to cool.

2 Place the tea leaves in a separate teapot, add the heated water, and leave to infuse for 3 minutes, then strain into a jug and leave to cool.

3 Pour the tea into the tumblers.

SERVE IT UP Add the ice cubes, stir, and garnish each with a slice of kumquat.

IRON GODDESS VODKA SERVES 2

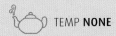 TEMP **NONE**　　 INFUSE **4-6 HRS**　　 TYPE **COCKTAIL**　　 MILK **WITHOUT**

It is fascinating to watch the tightly rolled Iron Goddess of Mercy opening in the vodka. The infusion is quite strong, so having some orange in the concoction helps to soften the blend.

2 tbsp **Iron Goddess of Mercy tea leaves** (Tie Guan Yin)

240ml (8fl oz) **vodka**

75ml (2½fl oz) **orange juice**

½ tsp **orange bitters**

ice cubes

a few thin rounds of **orange**, to garnish

Special equipment
cocktail shaker

1 Rinse the tea leaves with boiling water to help them unfurl more rapidly during infusion.

2 Place the tea leaves in a 400ml (14fl oz) lidded glass jug. Add the vodka and infuse for 4–6 hours. Strain the infusion into a cocktail shaker. Add the orange juice, bitters, and enough ice cubes to fill the shaker. Shake vigorously for a few seconds.

SERVE IT UP Strain into tumblers and garnish each with a round of orange.

ROCK ON! BOURBON SERVES 2

 TEMP **90°C (195°F)**　　 INFUSE **2 MINS**　　 TYPE **COCKTAIL**　　 MILK **WITHOUT**

Only a Southern whisky could stand up to the earthy flavours of Wuyi Rock. The smoky tones in the bourbon complement the roasted notes in the oolong tea, making this a bold drink.

5 tbsp **Wuyi Rock tea leaves**

300ml (10fl oz) **water** heated to 90°C (195°F)

90ml (3fl oz) **bourbon**

ice cubes

120ml (4fl oz) **soda water**

2 twists of **lemon rind**, to garnish

Special equipment
cocktail shaker

1 Place the tea leaves in a teapot, add the hot water, and infuse for 2 minutes. Strain into a cocktail shaker and leave to cool.

2 Add the bourbon and enough ice cubes to fill the shaker, and shake for 30 seconds.

SERVE IT UP Strain into cocktail glasses, add the soda water, and garnish each with a twist of lemon rind.

KOMBUCHA

This age-old fermented tea has become quite popular as a homebrew. Fizzy and slightly alcoholic, Kombucha has a sweet and sour taste that is clean and refreshing. With bacterial flora and healthy acids that promote intestinal health, this probiotic drink can be consumed as a daily tonic.

The origins of Kombucha can be traced back to China during the Han Dynasty (206BCE–25CE). From there it made its way to Russia through Mongolia in the 19th century. Around 1910, Kombucha arrived in Eastern Europe and was popular in Germany between the first and second World Wars, but became less so due to the scarcity of sugar and tea during WWII. Interest in Kombucha was revived in Europe and America during the 1990s and it has since become a popular beverage among homebrewers.

Kombucha is made by fermenting sweetened black or green tea with a culture of yeast and beneficial bacteria called a "kombucha mushroom", or SCOBY (see box, below). As the yeast in the SCOBY consumes the sugary tea, it produces a small amount of alcohol (less than 1 per cent) and CO_2 as by-products, which give Kombucha its sparkle. Although the alcohol content is very low, it is not recommended for children or women who are pregnant or breastfeeding.

DRINK TWO OR THREE SMALL GLASSES A DAY TO REAP THE HEALTH BENEFITS OF KOMBUCHA

THE SCOBY

The living ingredient in Kombucha is the SCOBY, an acronym for Symbiotic Colony Of Bacteria and Yeast. The SCOBY is similar to "mother of vinegar", the jelly-like layer that forms on top of apple cider vinegar and gives it sourness, but is much more solid. Slimy in texture and beige in colour, it will take on the shape of the container in which it is cultured. It requires the right conditions to turn tea and sugar into acetic acid (colourless liquid with an acidic taste) through fermentation. The SCOBY, or Kombucha liquid, should never come into contact with metal of any sort since the chemical reaction will damage the SCOBY and the culture in the liquid.

Assam tea

HOW TO MAKE

This effervescent beverage can be easily prepared at home, and is a good alternative to fizzy drinks, as it is lighter and contains acids and enzymes that aid digestion. All you need is a clean work area, some simple equipment, ingredients, and the willingness to wait for the tea to ferment.

1 Place the spring water in a large 4-litre (7-pint) saucepan and bring to the boil. Then remove from the heat, add the tea leaves, and steep for 5 minutes.

2 Strain the tea into the large glass jar and discard the tea leaves. Add the sugar and stir until it has dissolved. Cover the container loosely and leave to cool for several hours.

3 When the tea has cooled, add the shop-bought Kombucha, stirring with a wooden spoon. Wearing the gloves, place the SCOBY inside the jar. Cover the jar with the cloth, fastening it with an elastic band to keep out flies and moulds.

4 Leave the glass jar with the SCOBY and tea to sit undisturbed and away from sunlight for a week. The SCOBY will sink to the bottom as it ferments. After several days it will either rise to the top, or another SCOBY will start its culture at the top and grow thicker.

YOU WILL NEED

Ingredients

3.3 litres (5½ pints) spring water

8 tsp black loose-leaf tea

200g (7oz) cane sugar

500ml (16fl oz) unpasteurized, unflavoured shop-bought Kombucha (to use as "starter" liquid)

Kombucha SCOBY

Special equipment

4-litre (7-pint) sterile glass jar, plus 1-litre (1¾-pint) sterile glass jar

pair of new vinyl or latex gloves

piece of clean fineweave cloth, large enough to cover the top of the jar

elastic band

6 x 500ml (16fl oz) sterile bottles

1 plastic funnel

5 After fermentation, try a little sample with a wooden spoon to check the sparkle and flavour. It should have a light sparkle, like champagne, and taste like apple cider vinegar. If it is too sweet, leave it to ferment a little longer. The timing will need some experimentation, give or take a few days.

6 When the Kombucha is ready, remove the SCOBY and place it in the smaller glass jar. Pour over 750ml (1¼ pints) of the prepared Kombucha and close the lid. Refrigerate for up to 2 months until you are ready to start the next batch.

7 Pour the remaining Kombucha into the bottles through the plastic funnel. Close the lids and let them sit for a "secondary fermentation" for several days to add extra effervescence. Once fermented, store the bottles in the fridge. If you want to flavour it, just before bottling, add 1 part fresh or preserved fruit juice to 5 parts Kombucha.

SALTED CARAMEL ASSAM SERVES 4

 TEMP **100°C (210°F)**    INFUSE **5-6 MINS**   TYPE **HOT**    MILK **WHIPPED CREAM**

Salted caramel recipes usually call for a cooked sauce, but here is a cheat's version. Combining smoked salt and sugar with Assam's malty tones evokes the sweet and salty taste of this popular sauce.

3 tbsp **unsalted butter**

3 tbsp **cane sugar**

¼ tsp **smoked salt**

900ml (1½ pints) boiling **water**

3½ tbsp **Assam orthodox TGFOP tea leaves**

120ml (4fl oz) **whipped cream**, to serve

1 Place the butter, sugar, and the salt in a bowl, and pour over 175ml (6fl oz) boiling water. Mix to dissolve the sugar and salt, then set aside.

2 Place the tea leaves in a teapot, add the remaining water, and leave to infuse for 5-6 minutes.

3 Strain the tea into cups, add the salted caramel, and stir.

SERVE IT UP Top each cup with a dollop of whipped cream.

HONG KONG MILK TEA SERVES 4

 TEMP **100°C (210°F)**    INFUSE **1 MIN**   TYPE **HOT**   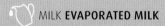 MILK **EVAPORATED MILK**

"Silk Stocking" tea became popular in Hong Kong in the 1950s. It is strained from one pot to another six times before milk and sugar are added. This was traditionally done using a long stocking-like cotton strainer, hence the nickname.

1 tbsp each of **Keemun, Assam, and Ceylon tea leaves**

3 tbsp **sugar**

2 x 175ml (6fl oz) small cans **evaporated milk**

1 Heat 900ml (1½ pints) water in a saucepan on a high heat and add the tea leaves. Boil for 1 minute, remove from the heat, and strain the tea into another saucepan.

2 Using the strainer with the residual tea leaves, strain the tea back into the first pan. Repeat the same process five times.

3 Add the sugar to the hot tea and stir well. Heat the milk in a saucepan. Do not boil. Remove from the heat and add to the tea.

SERVE IT UP Pour into cups and serve hot.

Hong Kong Milk Tea The smooth, creamy texture of this tea is the result of using evaporated milk.

CHOCOLATE FIG SERVES 4

 TEMP **100°C (210°F)**   INFUSE **5 MINS**   TYPE **HOT**   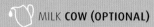 MILK **COW (OPTIONAL)**

The earthy flavours of Pu'er pair well with the sweetness of the black figs. Be sure to use dark chocolate with a high percentage of cocoa, or you will not get the full effect of the mix.

10 **dried black figs**

900ml (1½ pints) boiling **water**

20g (¾oz) **dark chocolate** (70 per cent or higher), finely chopped

4 tbsp **ripe Pu'er tea leaves**

1 Soak the figs in a little boiling water for 2 minutes to soften them. Cut into small pieces.

2 Place the chocolate in a teapot with the figs. Add 175ml (6fl oz) boiling water and stir.

3 Place the tea leaves in a separate teapot, add the remaining water, and leave to infuse for 5 minutes. Strain into the chocolate and fig infusion.

SERVE IT UP Strain into cups, add milk, if desired, and serve hot.

EARTHY
CREAMY
SWEET

TIBETAN PO CHA SERVES 4

 TEMP **100°C (210°F)**   INFUSE **1 MIN**   TYPE **HOT**   MILK **COW**

Traditionally made with creamy yak milk, the strong and salty Tibetan Po Cha is an acquired taste. You may reduce the salt and add a little more butter and milk if you want a creamier version.

2 tbsp **ripe Pu'er tea leaves**

¼ tsp **salt**

200ml (7fl oz) **whole milk** or **double cream**

3 tbsp **unsalted butter**

Special equipment
blender

1 Fill a saucepan with 650ml (1 pint) water, add the tea leaves, and bring to the boil on a medium heat.

2 Add the salt and boil for 1 minute. Remove the pan from the heat. Steep the tea for 1 minute and strain into another saucepan.

3 Stir in the milk and simmer on a low heat for 1 minute. Pour into the blender, add the butter, and blend until frothy.

SERVE IT UP Pour into serving bowls or mugs.

ORCHARD ROSE SERVES 4

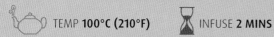 TEMP **100°C (210°F)** 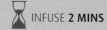 INFUSE **2 MINS** TYPE **HOT** 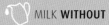 MILK **WITHOUT**

Cardamom and rosewater infuse the bright and lively Ceylon tea with an exotic flavour. Be careful not to steep for too long, as the tea can become astringent. The addition of honey and apple provides a welcome sweetness.

1 **apple**, cored and diced

seeds from 8 **cardamom pods**, crushed

1½ tsp **rosewater**

3 tsp **honey**

870ml (1½ pints) boiling **water**

3½ tbsp **Ceylon tea leaves**

4 **rosebuds** or thin **apple slices**, to garnish

1 Place the apple, cardamom, rosewater, and honey in a teapot. Pour over 175ml (6fl oz) boiling water and steep for 4 minutes.

2 Place the Ceylon tea leaves in a separate teapot, add the remaining water, and steep for 2 minutes.

3 Strain the tea into the apple infusion and steep for a further 3 minutes.

SERVE IT UP Strain into cups and garnish each with a rosebud or an apple slice before serving.

SPICY CEYLON SERVES 4

 TEMP **100°C (210°F)** INFUSE **2 MINS** TYPE **HOT** 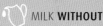 MILK **WITHOUT**

Some people enjoy Ceylon tea au naturel, while others like it sweetened with sugar or honey. Try this spicy version with just enough heat from the jalapeños to keep your tea warm, even as it starts to cool down.

zest of 1½ **limes**

7.5cm (3in) **jalapeño pepper**, sliced crossways, including seeds and membrane

900ml (1½ pints) boiling **water**

3 tbsp **Ceylon tea leaves**

4 slices of **lime**, to garnish

1 Place the lime zest and pepper in a teapot, add 200ml (7fl oz) boiling water, and leave to steep.

2 Place the tea leaves in a separate teapot, add the remaining water, and steep for 2 minutes.

3 Strain the tea into the pepper infusion and steep for a further 2 minutes.

SERVE IT UP Strain the infusion into cups and garnish each with a slice of lime.

ICED YUZU ASSAM SERVES 2

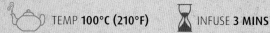 TEMP **100°C (210°F)**   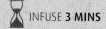 INFUSE **3 MINS**   TYPE **ICED**   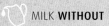 MILK **WITHOUT**

Yuzu, a zesty and light Asian citrus fruit, can be hard to find fresh, but is widely available preserved in jars from Asian stores. Simply rinse off the sugars and chop. Orange blossom water lightens the deep flavours of the Assam.

2 tbsp **yuzu peel** or a combination of orange and lemon peel

6 drops **orange blossom water**

2 tbsp **Assam tea leaves**

450ml (15fl oz) boiling **water**

ice cubes

Special equipment
muddler, or pestle

1 Divide the yuzu peel between 2 tumblers. Add 3 drops of the orange blossom water to each tumbler. Muddle the ingredients with a muddler or pestle.

2 Place the tea leaves in a teapot, add the boiling water, and steep for 3 minutes.

3 Strain the tea infusion into the yuzu mixture and leave to cool.

SERVE IT UP Add the ice cubes and stir before serving.

TEA GARDEN FROST SERVES 2

 TEMP **100°C (210°F)**   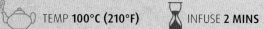 INFUSE **2 MINS**   TYPE **ICED**   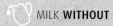 MILK **WITHOUT**

Ceylon tea is zesty and delicious on its own, but also blends well with different flavours from other ingredients. Basil's liquorice qualities shine through and persimmon adds a touch of sweetness.

2 tbsp **torn fresh basil leaves**, or 1 tbsp **dried basil leaves**

pinch of **lemon zest**

4 tbsp **diced fresh persimmon**, or 3 tbsp **diced dried persimmon**

2 tbsp **Ceylon tea leaves**

500ml (16fl oz) boiling **water**

ice cubes

Special equipment
muddler, or pestle

1 Divide the basil and lemon zest equally between 2 tumblers. Muddle them with a muddler or pestle.

2 Add the persimmon to the tumblers.

3 Place the tea leaves in a teapot, add the boiling water, and steep for 2 minutes.

4 Strain the tea into the fruit and basil mixture in the tumblers and leave to cool.

SERVE IT UP Add the ice cubes and serve.

MOUNTAIN FLUSH SERVES 2

 TEMP **NONE**   INFUSE **8 HRS**   TYPE **COLD**   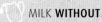 MILK **WITHOUT**

The beauty of cold infusion is that it allows the tea leaves to release their flavours slowly, thus yielding a sweeter taste. The Darjeeling tea's well-rounded character combines with the sweetness from the grapes to create a drink that's worth the wait.

15 **seedless green grapes**, sliced

3 tsp **Darjeeling tea leaves**
   (autumnal flush)

Special equipment
muddler, or pestle

1 Muddle half the grapes with a muddler or pestle, and place them along with the remaining grapes and tea leaves in a 750-ml (1¼-pint) lidded jug.

2 Pour over 500ml (16fl oz) cool water, stir, and cover. Then leave in the fridge for 8 hours.

SERVE IT UP Pour into 2 tumblers to serve.

ICED TIPPY YUNNAN SERVES 2

 TEMP **100°C (210°F)**   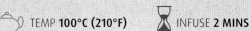 INFUSE **2 MINS**   TYPE **ICED**   MILK **WITHOUT**

Yunnan has a rich and deep flavour that complements the citrussy notes of orange. In small doses, orange and vanilla provide a rounded fruitiness to this iced drink.

½ tsp **orange zest**

1 tsp **caster sugar**

1cm (½in) **sliced vanilla bean**, or
   a few drops of **pure vanilla extract**

3 tsp **Yunnan Golden Tips tea leaves**

500ml (16fl oz) boiling **water**

ice cubes

2 **orange slices**, to garnish

1 Place the orange zest, sugar, and vanilla in a large heatproof glass jug.

2 Place the tea leaves in a teapot, add the boiling water, and steep for 2 minutes.

3 Strain the tea into the zest mixture in the jug. Stir and leave to cool.

SERVE IT UP When cool, add the ice cubes and pour into 2 tumblers. Garnish each with an orange slice.

SMOOTH **SWEET** CITRUS

MASALA CHAI

Masala Chai first emerged in colonial India and has grown to become a popular choice for tea drinkers all over the world. Varied combinations of spices bring an almost infinite variety to this delicious spiced hot beverage.

Chai wallahs (tea vendors) can be found on every street corner in India, sometimes in a small booth with a roof, sometimes squatting on the ground with nothing more than a pot and a tiny fire. Some of these tea vendors have perfected an elaborate preparation involving adding spice to milk and tea, and straining and pouring from one saucepan to the other from a height of several feet.

YOU WILL NEED

Ingredients

6 cloves

2 star anise

7.5cm (3in) cinnamon stick

5 cardamom pods

5cm (2in) piece fresh root ginger, sliced

1 heaped tbsp black Assam tea

400ml (16fl oz) buffalo or whole milk

3–4 tbsp sugar or honey, to taste

Special equipment
hand-held blender (optional)

1 Place all the spices, except the sliced ginger, in a mortar. Crush and grind them with a pestle until they break into small pieces and produce a warm and striking aromatic scent.

2 Place the crushed spices, sliced ginger, and tea leaves in a saucepan, and warm on a medium heat for 3–4 minutes to sweat the aromatics from the spices and the tea. Using a wooden spoon, stir frequently to ensure the mixture does not burn.

ASSAM TEA'S STRENGTH AND ASTRINGENCY ARE WELL SUITED TO STAND UP TO STRONG SPICES

3 Add 650ml (1 pint) water to the pan and bring to the boil on a high heat. Reduce the heat and let the tea simmer, all the while stirring with the spoon.

4 Add the milk and sugar and continue stirring. Simmer for a further 2 minutes, allowing all the ingredients to blend. Remove the pan from the heat and strain the tea into a teapot.

SERVE IT UP
Pour into mugs or cups from a height of at least 30cm (12in) to create foam on the surface.

CHAI FUSIONS

Use the Masala Chai recipe on pages 182–183 and adapt it to your taste with different blends of flavourings or spices. You can add chocolate, alcohol, or even chilli, if you like a little heat in your drink, but avoid acidic fruit as it will curdle the mixture.

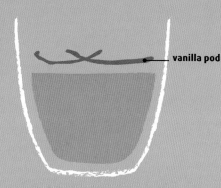

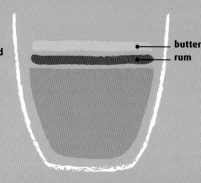

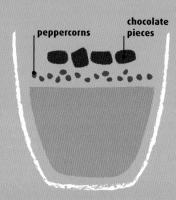

CHAI WITH VANILLA

Add two 2.5cm (1in) pieces of **vanilla pod**, split, just as the mixture starts to simmer. Alternatively, add a few drops of **vanilla or almond extract** at the end of the simmering.

HOT BUTTERED RUM CHAI

Add 2 tbsp **rum** and 1 tsp **butter** per serving, just as the tea is being served. Add more rum if you prefer it a little stronger.

CHAI WITH THE WORKS

This is a delicious blend of spices, pepper, and chocolate. Add ¼ tsp **black peppercorns** early on and 25g (scant 1oz) **dark chocolate** at the end. Adjust amounts based on your tolerance for heat. Add milk if you overdo it.

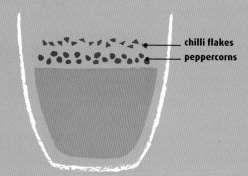

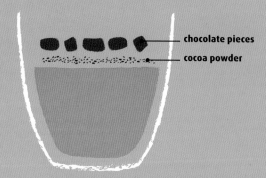

CHAI WITH HEAT

Add ¼ tsp **black peppercorns** or **chilli flakes** (or both) to the spices when crushing. Do not breathe too deeply or the heat might make you cough. It is not unusual to find peppercorns in some traditional Chai recipes, depending on the region.

CHOCOLATE CHAI

For an even richer dessert-style Chai, add 1 tbsp **unsweetened cocoa powder** or 15g (½oz) **chocolate** (2 large squares) at the end of the simmering, just before the tea is strained. For a creamy white chocolate Chai, add 20g (¾oz) **white chocolate** (3 large squares).

PREPARING CHAI WILL RELEASE DELICIOUS FRAGRANCES AND AROMAS IN YOUR KITCHEN

GREEN TEA CHAI

Green tea leaves are used in the Kashmiri area of India. They are easily available worldwide as an alternative to the dark and heavy Assam. Use fewer cloves and cinnamon, and a little more cardamom with green tea.

milk froth

milk

CHAI LATTÉ

Heat some **whole milk** separately and use either a hand-held blender or milk frother to create a foam that can be added to the top of the Chai. Try almond milk or coconut milk to replace cow's milk, if you prefer.

MASALA CHAI CONCENTRATE

How lovely to reach into the fridge and find the syrupy essence of Masala Chai ready to add to a smoothie or to make a quick iced Chai. Or, warm some milk and add a tablespoon or two, depending on how strong you like it. This concentrate is easy to make, but requires a bit of time for the tea to reduce to syrup.

Ingredients

3 tbsp Assam black tea leaves

1.2 litres (2 pints) water

75ml (2½fl oz) raw honey

1 vanilla pod, split

2 tsp grated ginger

5 whole cloves

10 crushed cardamom pods

1 tsp anise seeds

3 cinnamon sticks

1 tsp ground nutmeg

1 Place all the ingredients in a saucepan on a medium heat and simmer for about 30 minutes until reduced by about one-third.

2 Strain the liquid into a jar or bottle and allow to cool before storing in the fridge.

PEACHY ASSAM LATTÉ SERVES 2

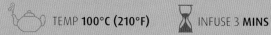 TEMP **100°C (210°F)** 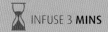 INFUSE 3 **MINS**  TYPE **LATTÉ** 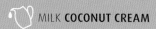 MILK **COCONUT CREAM**

Rich coconut cream is the best bet for this latté. The fruitiness of this mix needs some sweetening and the vanilla sugar works nicely. Try this as a dessert tea, or as an indulgent treat for a weekend brunch.

1 **ripe peach**, cored and sliced, or canned peach, rinsed

650ml (1 pint) boiling **water**

3 tbsp **Assam tea leaves**

6 tsp **vanilla-infused sugar**

150ml (5fl oz) top thick layer of **canned coconut cream**, plus 2 tbsp milk layer

Special equipment
hand-held blender

1 Place the peach slices in a teapot and add just enough boiling water to cover.

2 Place the tea leaves in a separate teapot, add the remaining water, and steep for 3 minutes. Strain into the peach infusion and steep for a further 2 minutes.

3 Pour into a bowl and add the sugar, coconut cream, and coconut milk. Using a hand-held blender, blend the peaches into the tea and create a nice froth.

SERVE IT UP Serve hot, topped with a little coconut cream.

SEVILLE ORANGE LATTÉ SERVES 2

 TEMP **100°C (210°F)** 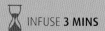 INFUSE 3 **MINS**  TYPE **LATTÉ** 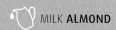 MILK **ALMOND**

Use a good-quality Seville orange marmalade for this recipe. Its sour and bitter taste will blend beautifully with the robust flavours of the Assam. Almond milk adds rich sweetness to the drink.

3 tbsp **Assam tea leaves**

650ml (1 pint) boiling **water**

240ml (8fl oz) **sweetened almond milk**

2 tbsp **Seville orange marmalade**

1 Place the tea leaves in a teapot, add boiling water, and steep for 3 minutes. Then strain the tea and discard all the tea leaves.

2 In a saucepan, warm the almond milk with the marmalade on a low heat until the marmalade melts.

3 Remove from the heat, strain the orange rinds, and pour into the teapot.

SERVE IT UP Pour into cups from a height to create froth, and serve immediately.

TANGY
CITRUS
SMOOTH

PU'ER CHOCOLATE SERVES 2

TEMP **100°C (210°F)`**   INFUSE **2 MINS**   TYPE **COCKTAIL**   MILK **WITHOUT**

Both chocolate and Pu'er have strong, deep flavours and are often paired together. In this recipe, Pu'er and chocolate bitters are added to white rum to create a wonderfully rich and velvety drink.

3 tbsp **Pu'er tea leaves**

400ml (14fl oz) boiling **water**

120ml (4fl oz) **white rum**

4 tsp **chocolate bitters**

ice cubes

Special equipment

cocktail shaker

1 Place the tea leaves in a teapot and pour over the boiling water. Leave to infuse for 2 minutes.

2 Pour into a cocktail shaker and leave to cool. Add the white rum, chocolate bitters, and enough ice cubes to fill the shaker.

SERVE IT UP Shake vigorously for a few seconds, strain into cocktail glasses, and serve.

FORTIFIED ASSAM SERVES 2

TEMP **100°C (210°F)**   INFUSE **3 MINS**   TYPE **COCKTAIL**   MILK **WITHOUT**

This drink, which is served as an aperitif, tastes like a fortified "tea wine". The reduction can be made with other black teas, and will keep well in the fridge for weeks, or in the freezer for six months. You can use it in iced tea, too.

1 tbsp **Assam tea leaves**

240ml (8fl oz) boiling **water**

3 tbsp **sugar**

175ml (6fl oz) **medium-dry sherry**

4 **twists of lemon**, to garnish

1 Place the tea leaves in a teapot, add the boiling water, and steep for 3 minutes.

2 Strain into a saucepan and add the sugar.

3 Boil the tea on a high heat for about 15 minutes, until the volume has reduced by two-thirds.

4 Allow the reduction to cool before adding the sherry.

SERVE IT UP Serve garnished with twists of lemon in sherry or wine glasses.

Keemun Alexander Creamy and malty, this chocolate-based cocktail is an indulgent evening treat.

KEEMUN ALEXANDER SERVES 2

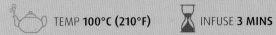 TEMP **100°C (210°F)**   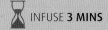 INFUSE **3 MINS**   TYPE **COCKTAIL**   MILK **DOUBLE CREAM**

This is a tribute to the classic gin cocktail, Alexander, which was invented around 1910. In this recipe, crème de cacao is replaced with chocolate bitters, malty Keemun, and double cream to create a deliciously rich cocktail.

2 tbsp **Keemun tea leaves**

400ml (14fl oz) boiling **water**

20g (¾oz) **dark chocolate**

120ml (4fl oz) **gin**

1 tsp **chocolate bitters**

3 tbsp **double cream**

1 Place the tea leaves in a teapot, add the boiling water, and steep for 3 minutes.

2 Strain into a jug, add the chocolate, and stir to melt. Allow to cool.

3 When cool, add the gin, chocolate bitters, and double cream, and stir until mixed.

SERVE IT UP Pour into cocktail glasses with sugared rims, and serve.

LONG ISLAND ICED TEA SERVES 2

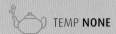 TEMP **NONE**   INFUSE **NONE**   TYPE **COCKTAIL**   MILK **WITHOUT**

The only thing tea-like about this classic American drink is the colour. It looks like iced tea, but do not be fooled as this heady drink does not have the slightest hint of tea in it.

30ml (1fl oz) each of **gin, tequila, vodka, white rum, triple sec, and simple syrup**

60ml (2fl oz) **lemon** juice

120ml (4fl oz) **cola**

ice cubes

2 **lemon wedges**, to garnish

Special equipment
cocktail shaker

1 Pour all the liquid ingredients, except for the cola, into a cocktail shaker. Add enough ice cubes to fill the shaker, then shake vigorously for a few seconds.

2 Strain into tall Collins glasses filled with ice, and top up with cola.

SERVE IT UP Decorate with a wedge of lemon in each glass, and serve.

PU'ER SANGRIA SERVES 4

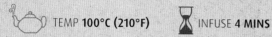 TEMP **100°C (210°F)**   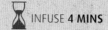 INFUSE **4 MINS**   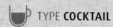 TYPE **COCKTAIL**   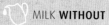 MILK **WITHOUT**

The wonderful thing about Sangria is that you can make it ahead of time as it improves after sitting in the fridge for a few hours. The fruit soaks up the wine, cognac, and Pu'er, creating a fruit ambrosia. Have your spoons at the ready!

1 **peach**, cored and sliced

12 **strawberries**, sliced

1 **orange**, segmented

2 tbsp **Pu'er tea leaves**

240ml (8fl oz) boiling **water**

75ml (2½fl oz) **Grand Marnier**

400ml (14fl oz) **red wine**

ice cubes

1 Place the fruits in a 1.4-litre (2½-pint) glass jug.

2 Place the tea leaves in a teapot, add the boiling water, and steep for 4 minutes.

3 Leave to cool and pour into the jug. Add the Grand Marnier, wine, and ice cubes, and stir.

SERVE IT UP Serve in wine glasses.

MONSOON SEASON SERVES 4

 TEMP **100°C (210°F)**   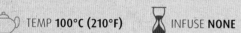 INFUSE **NONE**   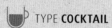 TYPE **COCKTAIL**   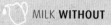 MILK **WITHOUT**

In this boozy take on classic tea with lemon, the Ceylon reduction provides a zesty tea flavour, which stands up to the addition of vodka. Limoncello replicates the tart and sweet flavours of lemon and sugar.

4 tbsp Ceylon reduction:

   1 tbsp **Ceylon tea leaves**

   240ml (8fl oz) boiling **water**

   3 tbsp **sugar**

60ml (2fl oz) each **vodka** and **limoncello**

ice cubes

200ml (7fl oz) **soda water**

4 **lemon slices**, to garnish

Special equipment
cocktail shaker

1 To prepare the Ceylon reduction, follow the directions for the Assam reduction on page 187.

2 Place the vodka and limoncello in a cocktail shaker with the Ceylon reduction, and shake vigorously for 1 minute.

SERVE IT UP Strain into cocktail glasses half-filled with ice and add the soda water. Serve with a lemon slice garnish in each.

FRAGRANT PAGODA SERVES 4

 TEMP **80°C (175°F)**   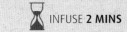 INFUSE **2 MINS**   TYPE **HOT**   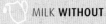 MILK **WITHOUT**

This rare yellow tea comes from Dongting Lake in Hunan province. It is a delicate tea so this recipe is light on flavouring. The few drops of elderflower cordial make an impression, but allow the sweet flavour of the tea to come through.

3 tbsp **Jun Shan Yin Zhen tea leaves**

900ml (1½ pints) **water** heated to 80°C (175°F)

10 drops **elderflower cordial**

1 Place the tea leaves in a teapot and add the hot water. Leave to steep for 2 minutes.

2 Just before straining the infusion, add the elderflower cordial. Set aside a few tea leaves to garnish.

SERVE IT UP Strain into cups or mugs, and serve garnished with the reserved tea leaves.

SWEET
DELICATE
MILD

SUMMER PALACE SERVES 2

 TEMP **80°C (175°F)**    INFUSE **2 MINS**   TYPE **ICED**   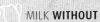 MILK **WITHOUT**

Huo Shan Huang Ya is a light and graceful tea that has a slightly toasty edge. Put it on ice and it becomes a light and clean thirst quencher, with an apple-like sweetness that comes from the star fruit. This delicate drink is grassy and fruity.

1 **star fruit,** sliced, plus 2 thin slices, to garnish

100ml (3½fl oz) boiling **water,** plus 400ml (14fl oz) water heated to 80°C (175°F)

1 tbsp **Huo Shan Huang Ya tea leaves**

2 tsp **honey**

ice cubes

1 Place the star fruit in a teapot. Add the boiling water and steep for 1 minute.

2 Add the tea leaves and the heated water to the teapot and steep for a further 2 minutes.

3 Strain the infusion into 2 tumblers and stir in the honey. Leave to cool. Add the ice cubes and stir.

SERVE IT UP Serve garnished with a slice of star fruit.

BUBBLE TEA

This flavoured fruit or milk tea gets its name from its chewy tapioca bubbles, also known as "boba", which add texture, sweetness, and visual appeal. Bubble tea originated in Taiwan in the early 1980s and has since gained popularity worldwide as a versatile and fun beverage.

HOW TO MAKE TARO BUBBLE TEA

This popular frothy drink gets its lovely purple colour and milkshake-like consistency from its fibrous taro liquid base. Tapioca pearls add a fun element to this easy recipe. Made from tapioca starch, these soft, chewy, and slightly sweet bubbles sink to the bottom of the tumbler and can only be drawn up through a fat straw.

YOU WILL NEED

Ingredients

150g (5½oz) 5-minute tapioca pearls (will yield enough for 4 servings)

225g (8oz) caster sugar

200g (7oz) taro root, peeled and chopped

honey or sugar, to sweeten

Special equipment

hand-held blender

1 In a large saucepan, bring 2 litres (3½ pints) of water to the boil and add the tapioca pearls. Simmer for 1–2 minutes until the pearls rise to the surface and start to soften. Reduce to a medium heat, cover, and simmer for 5 minutes.

2 Remove the tapioca pearls with a slotted spoon and place in a bowl of cold water to prevent them from sticking together. Boil 240ml (8fl oz) water with the sugar for 2 minutes. Cool, then soak the pearls in the sugar syrup for 15 minutes.

3 For the taro liquid, boil the taro root in 480ml (16fl oz) water for 20 minutes, or until soft. Remove from the heat and drain. Blend the taro, adding fresh water, or milk, to get to drinking consistency. Sweeten to taste with honey or sugar. Pour into 2 tumblers and add one-quarter of the prepared tapioca pearls to each.

TARO ROOT
The versatile taro root can be roasted, boiled, or baked, and is rich in potassium and fibre.

Taro Bubble Tea This delightful drink is best enjoyed with freshly made tapioca boba.

HOW TO MAKE "POPPING" SPHERES

Spherification is the culinary process of shaping liquids into spheres. This molecular gastronomy technique has now made its way to the popular world of bubble tea, and can be used to experiment with a wide range of juices and teas to create "popping" spheres, or bubbles, to use instead of traditional tapioca.

YOU WILL NEED

Ingredients

6g sodium alginate powder

10g (¼oz) calcium chloride powder

juices, tisanes, or teas to flavour the alginate

Special equipment

hand-held blender

syringe or squeeze bottle

1 In a deep bowl, add the sodium alginate to 650ml (1 pint) water. Blend for 5–10 minutes. Transfer to a 2-litre (3½-pint) cooking pot and bring to the boil. Remove from the heat and transfer back to the bowl to cool completely.

2 In a separate bowl, mix 2 parts juice or strong tea with 3 parts cooled alginate. In another deep bowl, dissolve the calcium chloride in 2 litres (3½ pints) of water by stirring for 1–2 minutes; this will create a colourless liquid.

You could reduce the quantities in the recipe by half if you don't want to spend too much time making spheres.

3 Using a syringe or squeeze bottle, release droplets of the alginate mixture into the bowl containing the calcium chloride solution, one drop at a time.

4 Remove the spheres with a slotted spoon. Serve immediately as they will solidify within a few hours. Pour 500ml (16fl oz) tea of your choice into 2 tumblers and add one-quarter of the popping spheres to each.

Popping spheres Bite-sized balls filled with juice or flavoured liquid add an element of surprise to any bubble tea.

BUBBLE TEA FLAVOURS

Once you learn how to make the traditional bubble tea on page 192, you can start to experiment with a wealth of different flavour combinations. Try different teas, tisanes, and fruit infusions to see how versatile this drink is. Here are a few variations to help you get started.

froth

Assam tea, mango, and honey blend

clear tapioca boba

MANGO WITH BLACK TEA

Use the full-bodied **Assam tea** and blend with **mango**. Add **raw honey** to taste. Serve with **clear tapioca boba**. Mangolicious!

froth

pineapple and coconut water blend

pineapple juice boba

PINEAPPLE WITH COCONUT

Blend **pineapple** pieces with **coconut water** and add **pineapple juice bursting boba**.

traditional Chai

chocolate milk boba

CHAI

Make some **traditional Chai**, but for a little surprise add **chocolate milk bursting boba**.

Matcha in mint tea

mint tea boba

MATCHA MINT

Whisk some **Matcha powder** into **mint tea**. Add **mint tea bursting boba**.

cocoa powder, almond milk, and honey

tapioca boba

CHOCOLATE WITH ALMOND MILK

Mix **unsweetened cocoa powder** with warm **almond milk** and **raw honey**. Add **tapioca boba**.

oolong tea

apricot juice boba

IRON GODDESS OF MERCY (TIE GUAN YIN) OOLONG

Add **apricot juice bursting boba** to this fragrant **oolong tea**.

BASIC PROPORTIONS
Makes 2 tumblers
500ml (16fl oz) prepared tea
240ml (8fl oz) fruit purée (if specified)
240ml (8fl oz) boba
6 ice cubes (if specified)

THE CHEWY BOBA ADD TEXTURE AND INTEREST TO THIS FILLING DRINK

- Gunpowder green tea and coconut milk
- coconut milk boba

GUNPOWDER GREEN WITH COCONUT

Mix **Gunpowder green tea** with **coconut milk**. Add **coconut milk boba**.

- Longevity White tea and rice milk
- pear juice boba

LONGEVITY WHITE WITH RICE MILK

Mix **Longevity White tea** (Bai Mu Dan) with warmed **sweetened rice milk** and add **pear juice bursting boba**.

- chamomile infusion and almond milk
- pineapple juice boba

CHAMOMILE WITH ALMOND MILK

Mix a prepared **chamomile infusion** with warmed **almond milk** and add **pineapple juice bursting boba**.

- peppermint honey infusion
- ice cubes
- lemonade boba

HONEY PEPPERMINT

Blend **peppermint infusion** with **ice cubes** and **raw honey**. Add **lemonade bursting boba**.

- froth
- chamomile infusion, orange, pineapple, and honey blend
- ice cubes
- coconut milk boba

ORANGE, PINEAPPLE, AND CHAMOMILE

Blend **chamomile infusion** and **fruits** with **ice cubes** and **raw honey**. Add **coconut milk boba**.

- ginger in almond milk
- ginger ale boba

GINGER WITH ALMOND MILK

Heat **sweetened almond milk** with **chopped ginger**. Strain and add **ginger ale bursting boba**.

ZESTY TULSI SERVES 4

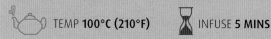 TEMP **100°C (210°F)**   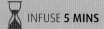 INFUSE **5 MINS**   TYPE **HOT**    MILK **WITHOUT**

Tulsi, or holy basil, has spicy and sweet flavours that are reminiscent of black peppercorns and anise. When combined with orange and cinnamon, it bursts with piquant tanginess.

3 **cinnamon sticks**, each 7.5cm (3in) long, crushed or broken

3 tsp **orange zest**, plus 4 orange slices, to garnish

870ml (1½ pints) boiling **water**

4 tbsp **tulsi leaves**

1 Place the cinnamon and orange zest in a teapot. Add 120ml (4fl oz) boiling water and set aside.

2 Place the tulsi leaves in a separate teapot, add the remaining water, and infuse for 5 minutes.

3 Strain the tulsi liquid into the cinnamon and orange infusion.

SERVE IT UP Strain the infusion into mugs, and serve with an orange slice garnish in each.

TANGY
SPICY
WARMING

APPLE GINGER ROOIBOS SERVES 4

 TEMP **100°C (210°F)**   INFUSE **6 MINS**   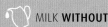 TYPE **HOT**   MILK **WITHOUT**

Rooibos has a fruity character that is brought out with the addition of fruits and spices. Fresh ginger and apple add sweetness and a little zip. This tea will do wonders for a sore throat or as a caffeine-free evening refresher.

1 **apple**, cored and diced, plus 4 thin slices, to garnish

½ tsp **grated ginger**

870ml (1½ pints) boiling **water**

3 tbsp **rooibos leaves**

1 Place the apple and ginger in a teapot. Pour over 120ml (4fl oz) boiling water and set aside to infuse.

2 Place the rooibos leaves in a separate teapot, add the remaining water, and infuse for 6 minutes.

3 Strain the rooibos infusion into the fruit infusion and leave for 1 minute.

SERVE IT UP Strain into cups or mugs, and serve with an apple slice garnish in each.

BAY SIDE VILLA SERVES 4

 TEMP **100°C (210°F)**  INFUSE **5 MINS** TYPE **HOT**  MILK **WITHOUT**

The herb bay laurel, commonly used in Mediterranean cuisine, has a savoury herbal flavour. Snack on the luscious bay-infused figs once the sweet and fruity herbal tea is poured.

8 **figs**, cut into slices

3 **fresh** or **dried bay leaves**, torn

pinch of **liquorice root powder**

900ml (1½ pints) boiling **water**

Special equipment
muddler, or pestle

1 Muddle the figs in a bowl with a muddler or pestle.

2 Place the figs and bay leaves in a teapot. Add the liquorice powder and pour over the boiling water. Leave to steep for 5 minutes.

SERVE IT UP Strain into cups and serve hot.

ROASTED CHICORY MOCHA SERVES 4

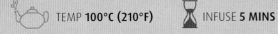 TEMP **100°C (210°F)** INFUSE **5 MINS** TYPE **HOT**  MILK **COW (OPTIONAL)**

Cacao nibs are slightly bitter in their raw form, but full of antioxidants, while roasted chicory, long used as a coffee substitute, helps to remove toxins from the body and aids digestion. Their combined goodness makes for a potent drink.

2 tbsp **coarsely ground roasted chicory root**

12 **raw cacao nibs**, crushed

900ml (1½ pints) boiling **water**

honey or **sugar**, to taste

4 squares **dark chocolate**, to serve

1 Place the roasted chicory and cacao nibs (including husks) in a teapot.

2 Add the boiling water and leave to infuse for 4 minutes.

3 Strain the infusion into cups or mugs and sweeten with honey or sugar to taste.

SERVE IT UP Serve each with a square of dark chocolate.

RASPBERRY LEMON VERBENA SERVES 4

 TEMP 100°c (210°f)    INFUSE 4 MINS   TYPE HOT   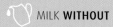 MILK WITHOUT

The raspberries create a beautiful shade of coral, and together with the verbena, which is calming, soothing, and a natural tonic that aids digestion, endows this tisane with goodness. The lemon flavour is tangy but not acidic.

10 large **raspberries**, fresh or frozen, plus 4 extra, to garnish

3 tbsp **dried lemon verbena leaves**

900ml (1½ pints) boiling **water**

Special equipment
muddler, or pestle

1 Place the raspberries in a teapot and muddle them using a muddler or pestle.

2 Add the lemon verbena leaves and pour over the boiling water. Infuse for 4 minutes.

SERVE IT UP Strain into cups or mugs, and garnish each with a raspberry.

REDBUSH MEADOW SERVES 4

 TEMP 100°C (210°F)   INFUSE 4 MINS   TYPE HOT   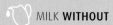 MILK WITHOUT

In this classic herbal infusion, all the ingredients are dried. Chamomile and lavender will calm, soothe, and relax. Rooibos, bursting with antioxidants, provides the strong base flavours and a beautiful coppery colour to the drink.

1 tbsp **rooibos leaves**

3 tbsp **chamomile flowers**, plus extra, to garnish

about 30 **lavender flower buds**, plus extra, to garnish

900ml (1½ pints) boiling **water**

1 Place the rooibos leaves and the chamomile and lavender flowers in a teapot and add the boiling water. Infuse for 4 minutes.

2 Strain the infusion into cups or mugs.

SERVE IT UP Garnish each with a few lavender and chamomile flowers.

RELAXING
CALMING
AROMATIC

Raspberry Lemon Verbena
A delightfully coloured tea that is tangy, fruity, and calming at the same time.

SPRING IS HERE SERVES 4

 TEMP **100°C (210°F)**    INFUSE **5 MINS**   TYPE **HOT**    MILK **WITHOUT**

Elderflower has a very strong perfume so only a small amount is needed in this tisane. The mulberry leaves act as a natural sweetener. Together these two herbs strike a delicate balance.

5 tbsp **dried mulberry leaves**

2 tsp **dried elderflower**

900ml (1½ pints) boiling **water**

1 Place the mulberry leaves and elderflower in a teapot.

2 Add the boiling water and leave to steep for 5 minutes.

SERVE IT UP Strain into cups or mugs, and serve hot.

SOOTHING
SWEET
DELICATE

FENNEL, LEMONGRASS, AND PEAR SERVES 4

 TEMP **100°C (210°F)**   INFUSE **5 MINS**   TYPE **HOT**   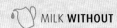 MILK **WITHOUT**

Lemongrass is a powerful antioxidant, while fennel is an all-purpose herb as it aids digestion, acts as an anti-inflammatory, and is a great detox remedy. Together they add potency to this sweet and refreshing drink.

1 **pear**, cored and sliced

1½ tsp dried **lemongrass**

1 tsp **fennel seeds**

900ml (1½ pints) boiling **water**

Special equipment

muddler, or pestle

1 Muddle half the pear slices with a muddler or pestle. Place them in a teapot along with the remaining pear, lemongrass, and fennel seeds.

2 Add the boiling water and leave to steep for 5 minutes.

SERVE IT UP Strain the infusion into cups or mugs, and serve hot.

BAMBOO LEAF, CHAMOMILE, AND PINEAPPLE SERVES 4

 TEMP **100°C (210°F)**    INFUSE **5 MINS**   TYPE **HOT**    MILK **WITHOUT**

Bamboo leaves are as light as a feather, and impart a beautiful green to the cup. It is a refreshing alternative to green tea when you don't want caffeine. Adding pineapple enhances the naturally fruity flavours of chamomile.

8 tbsp **dried bamboo leaves**, plus extra, to garnish

1 tbsp **dried chamomile flowers**

65g (2¼oz) **pineapple**, diced

900ml (1½ pints) boiling **water**

1 Place the bamboo leaves, chamomile, and pineapple in a teapot.

2 Add the boiling water and steep for 5 minutes.

SERVE IT UP Strain into white porcelain cups to show off the bright green infusion. Garnish with some bamboo leaves, and serve hot.

ROSEHIP, GINGER, AND LEMON SERVES 4

 TEMP **100°C (210°F)**   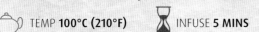 INFUSE **5 MINS**   TYPE **HOT**   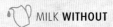 MILK **WITHOUT**

This blend contains classic ingredients that have great health benefits. Rosehips are packed with vitamin C, while ginger and lemon are fantastic cold-busters and possess anti-inflammatory qualities.

20g (¾oz) **dried rosehips** (about 25), crushed

½ tsp **grated ginger**

½ tsp **lemon zest**, plus 4 thin lemon slices, to garnish

900ml (1½ pints) boiling **water**

honey, to garnish (optional)

1 Place the rosehips, ginger, and lemon zest in a teapot, and add the boiling water.

2 Steep for 5 minutes, then strain into cups or mugs.

SERVE IT UP Garnish with a lemon slice in each, add honey if desired, and serve hot.

SOOTHING
TANGY
FRUITY

ROSY ROOIBOS SERVES 2

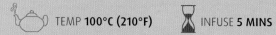 TEMP **100°C (210°F)** 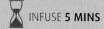 INFUSE **5 MINS**   TYPE **ICED** 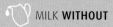 MILK **WITHOUT**

Easy does it with rooibos when mixing it with other flavours. It imparts a beautiful dark amber colour, though, and in this case mingles happily with the rosebuds and vanilla.

2 tbsp slightly crushed **rosebuds**

1 tbsp **rooibos leaves**

2½cm (1in) **vanilla pod**, split in half

500ml (16fl oz) boiling **water**

ice cubes

1 Reserve 2 rosebuds for garnishing. Place the remaining rosebuds, rooibos leaves, and vanilla pod in a teapot. Add the boiling water and leave to infuse for 5 minutes.

2 Strain into glass tea cups and allow to cool.

SERVE IT UP Add the ice cubes, stir, and serve with a rosebud garnish in each.

COOL AS A CUCUMBER SERVES 2

 TEMP **100°C (210°F)** 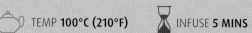 INFUSE **5 MINS**   TYPE **ICED** 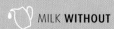 MILK **WITHOUT**

The ingredients suggest the best of summer. For this recipe, it is preferable to use fresh basil and mint as the infusion will not be as lively using dried herbs. The clean taste is cooling and thirst-quenching.

1 tbsp **torn mint leaves**

1 tbsp **torn basil leaves**

½ **cucumber**, sliced

500ml (16fl oz) boiling **water**

ice cubes

Special equipment
muddler, or pestle

1 Muddle the mint and basil leaves with a muddler or pestle to release their juices.

2 Place the leaves in a teapot, add the boiling water, and steep for 5 minutes. Leave to cool.

3 Divide the cucumber slices between 2 tumblers, and pour over the cooled infusion.

SERVE IT UP Add the ice cubes before serving.

Rosy Rooibos Fragrant and sweet, this caffeine-free iced tisane is as delicious as it is lovely looking.

MAY TO SEPTEMBER SERVES 2

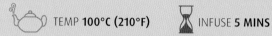 TEMP **100°C (210°F)**  INFUSE **5 MINS**   TYPE **ICED** 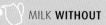 MILK **WITHOUT**

Elderflowers bloom at the beginning of summer, while elderberries signal summer's end, so only a dry version of each will work here. The crystalline garnet colour of the berries offers an elegant iced tea for warm autumn days.

1 tbsp **dried elderflowers**

1¼ tsp **dried elderberries**

500ml (16fl oz) boiling **water**

1 tsp **honey**

ice cubes

1 Place the elderflowers and elderberries in a teapot. Add the boiling water and infuse for 5 minutes.

2 Strain into a glass jug, stir in the honey, and allow to cool. Set aside a few of the infused elderflowers for garnishing.

SERVE IT UP Pour into 2 tumblers, add the ice cubes, and stir. Garnish each with the reserved elderflowers.

RED CLOVER, RED CLOVER! SERVES 2

 TEMP **100°C (210°F)** 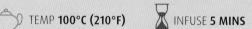 INFUSE **5 MINS**   TYPE **ICED** 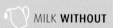 MILK **WITHOUT**

Chamomile has a concentrated sweetness and a dominant aroma. Only a small amount is used here to avoid overpowering the flavour of the clover blossoms. Both are calming herbs, and apple has anti-inflammatory benefits.

1 tbsp **dried chamomile flowers**

3 tbsp **dried red clover blossoms**, broken apart slightly

1 large **apple**, finely diced, plus 4 thin slices, to garnish

500ml (16fl oz) boiling **water**

ice cubes

1 Place the chamomile and red clover blossoms with the apple in a teapot. Add the boiling water and leave to steep for 5 minutes.

2 Strain the infusion into a glass jug and allow to cool.

SERVE IT UP Pour into 2 tumblers, add the ice cubes, and stir. Serve garnished with the apple slices.

ICY GINGER YERBA MATE SERVES 2

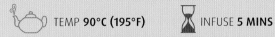 TEMP **90°C (195°F)**    INFUSE **5 MINS**   TYPE **ICED**   MILK **WITHOUT**

Traditionally, South American yerba mate is served in a gourd cup, sipped through a bombilla straw, and passed from guest to guest. Here is an easy iced version with a little zing from ginger and honey.

2 tbsp **yerba mate leaves**

½ tsp **grated ginger root**

500ml (16fl oz) **water** heated to 90°C (195°F)

1 tsp **honey**

ice cubes

1 Place the leaves and ginger in a teapot. Add the hot water and steep for 5 minutes.

2 Strain into a glass jug. Add the honey and stir. Leave to cool, then chill in the fridge.

SERVE IT UP Pour into 2 tumblers and add the ice cubes.

ANISE AND BLACK CHERRY SERVES 2

 TEMP **100°C (210°F)**   INFUSE **5 MINS**   TYPE **ICED**   MILK **WITHOUT**

Anise is naturally sweet and has a pronounced liquorice flavour, which combines well with the fruit sugars in the black cherries, and adds an unexpected spice to this fruity drink.

20 **black cherries**, fresh or frozen, pitted and halved, plus extra, to garnish

1 tsp **anise seeds**

500ml (16fl oz) boiling **water**

ice cubes

Special equipment
muddler, or pestle

1 Muddle the cherries in a teapot with a muddler or pestle. Add the anise seeds and the boiling water, then steep for 5 minutes.

2 Strain the infusion into a glass jug, allow to cool, then chill.

3 Add the ice cubes and stir.

SERVE IT UP Pour into 2 tumblers and garnish with the extra cherries.

STONE FRUITS **SWEET** LIQUORICE

ICED LIME MATE SERVES 2

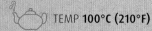 TEMP **100°C (210°F)**   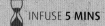 INFUSE **5 MINS**   TYPE **ICED**   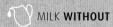 MILK **WITHOUT**

This ancient South American herb is a member of the holly family. It has a slightly bitter taste, but some traditionalists wouldn't dream of sweetening it. Here, the liquorice sweetens and the lime harmonizes the flavours.

2 tbsp **yerba mate leaves**

½ tsp **ground liquorice root**

1 tsp **lime zest**, plus 2 thin lime slices, to garnish

500ml (16fl oz) boiling **water**

ice cubes

1 Place the leaves, liquorice root, and lime zest in a teapot. Add the boiling water and leave to infuse for 5 minutes.

2 Strain into a glass jug and leave to cool.

SERVE IT UP Pour into 2 tumblers, add the ice cubes, and stir. Garnish each with a lime slice.

SWEET SMOKE CITRUS

ROSY CITRUS FROST SERVES 2

 TEMP **100°C (210°F)**   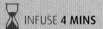 INFUSE **4 MINS**   TYPE **ICED**   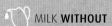 MILK **WITHOUT**

Hibiscus is often found in herbal blends because of the beautiful deep red colour it releases in the infusion. Honey tones down the tartness of the rosehips and hibiscus. A fantastic tonic, digestive, and cold buster.

1 tsp **dried hibiscus flowers** (Flor de Jamaica)

8 whole **rosehips**, crushed

3 whole **cloves**

1 tsp **orange zest**, plus 2 slices of orange, to garnish

500ml (16fl oz) boiling **water**

4 tsp **honey**

ice cubes

1 Place the hibiscus and rosehips in a teapot with the cloves and orange zest.

2 Add the boiling water and leave to steep for 4 minutes.

3 Strain into a glass jug, add the honey, and stir. Leave to cool.

SERVE IT UP Pour into 2 tumblers filled with ice cubes and serve garnished with orange slices.

CRÈME DE CASSIS SERVES 2

 TEMP **100°C (210°F)**    INFUSE **5 MINS**    TYPE **COCKTAIL**    MILK **WITHOUT**

A sweet, dark liqueur made from blackcurrants, crème de cassis gives a distinctly sweet flavour to the drink. Fennel, popular in Mediterranean cuisine, delivers the wow factor with its liquorice kick.

3 tbsp **crushed fennel seeds**

400ml (14fl oz) boiling **water**

60ml (2fl oz) **vodka**

60ml (2fl oz) **crème de cassis**

ice cubes

Special equipment

cocktail shaker

1 Place the fennel seeds in a teapot, add the boiling water, and leave to infuse for 5 minutes.

2 Strain into the cocktail shaker and leave to cool.

3 Add the vodka, crème de cassis, and enough ice cubes to fill the cocktail shaker. Shake vigorously for 30 seconds.

SERVE IT UP Strain into 2 cocktail glasses.

SOUTHERN VERANDA SERVES 2

 TEMP **100°C (210°F)**   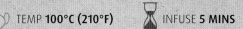 INFUSE **5 MINS**   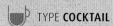 TYPE **COCKTAIL**   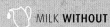 MILK **WITHOUT**

Chamomile has a distinctive pineapple scent that is perfectly set off by the smokiness of the bourbon. This fragrant cocktail spells sweet indulgence on a summer evening.

5 tbsp **dried chamomile flowers**

400ml (14fl oz) boiling **water**

120ml (4fl oz) **bourbon**

½ tsp **lavender bitters**

ice cubes

Special equipment

cocktail shaker

1 Place the chamomile flowers in a teapot, add the boiling water, and leave to infuse for 5 minutes. Strain into the cocktail shaker and allow to cool.

2 Add the bourbon, lavender bitters, and enough ice cubes to fill the cocktail shaker. Shake vigorously for a few seconds.

SERVE IT UP Strain into 2 cocktail glasses.

ROOIBOOZE SERVES 2

 TEMP **100°C (210°F)**   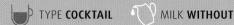 INFUSE **5 MINS**   TYPE **COCKTAIL**   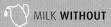 MILK **WITHOUT**

Spin the classic martini into a "teatini" or "mar-tea-ni". Combine the signature juniper taste of gin with a sweet vermouth rather than the usual dry vermouth. Rooibos is so fruity, why fight it?

2 tbsp **rooibos leaves**

400ml (14fl oz) boiling **water**

60ml (2fl oz) **gin**

60ml (2fl oz) **sweet vermouth**

ice cubes

4 twists of **lime rind**, to garnish

Special equipment
cocktail shaker

1 Place the rooibos leaves in a teapot, add the boiling water, and leave to infuse for 5 minutes.

2 Strain into the cocktail shaker and leave to cool.

3 Add the gin, vermouth, and enough ice cubes to fill the shaker, then shake vigorously for a few seconds.

SERVE IT UP Strain into cocktail glasses and serve garnished with the twists of lime rind.

LEMON YERBACELLO SERVES 2

 TEMP **100°C (210°F)**   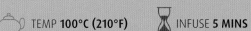 INFUSE **5 MINS**   TYPE **COCKTAIL**   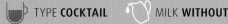 MILK **WITHOUT**

Some describe yerba as tasting like green tea, but it also has a slight tobacco aroma, which blends pleasantly with limoncello. Be sure to add ice, though, because this is a sweet one.

3 tbsp **yerba mate leaves**

400ml (14fl oz) boiling **water**

120ml (4fl oz) **limoncello**

ice cubes

4 twists of **lemon rind**, to garnish

Special equipment
cocktail shaker

1 Place the yerba mate leaves in a teapot, add the boiling water, and leave to infuse for 5 minutes.

2 Strain into the cocktail shaker and leave to cool.

3 Add the limoncello and enough ice cubes to fill the shaker, and shake vigorously for a few seconds.

SERVE IT UP Strain into 2 cocktail glasses and serve garnished with the twists of lemon rind.

Rooibooze A fun twist on the classic martini – herbal, citrus, and fruity.

ORANGE SPICE SMOOTHIE SERVES 2

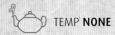 TEMP **NONE**   INFUSE **NONE**   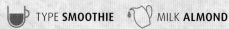 TYPE **SMOOTHIE**   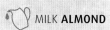 MILK **ALMOND**

Cool and citrussy, this creamy smoothie is loaded with vitamin C. The detoxifying and soothing qualities of orange zest and ginger are just what you want from a morning pick-me-up.

juice of 1 **orange**, plus 1 tsp **grated orange zest**

½ tsp **grated root ginger**

350ml (12fl oz) **plain low-fat yogurt**

2 tsp **hemp seeds**

120ml (4fl oz) **sweetened almond milk**

Special equipment
blender

1 Place the orange juice and zest, ginger, yogurt, and hemp seeds in a blender and blend well.

2 Add the almond milk into the blender and blend until the mixture is creamy.

SERVE IT UP Pour into 2 tumblers and serve immediately.

SPICY CREAMY CITRUSSY

OSMANTHUS FRAPPÉ SERVES 2

 TEMP **100°C (210°F)**   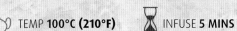 INFUSE **5 MINS**    TYPE **FRAPPÉ**    MILK **WITHOUT**

Osmanthus flowers, prized for their sweet and soothing aroma, are often added to green teas. Here they make a memorable pairing with lychee fruit, creating a drink that is frothy yet light.

1 tbsp **dried osmanthus flowers**

240ml (8fl oz) boiling **water**

4 tbsp **canned lychee syrup**

8 **lychees** from a can

240ml (8fl oz) **coconut water**

4 **ice cubes**

Special equipment
blender

1 Place the osmanthus flowers in a teapot, add the boiling water, and infuse for 5 minutes. Leave to cool.

2 Strain the infusion into a blender. Add the lychee syrup and fruit, and coconut water, and blend until smooth.

3 Add the ice cubes and blend until crushed.

SERVE IT UP Pour into 2 tumblers and serve immediately.

FRUITY FROTH SERVES 2

 TEMP **NONE**   INFUSE **NONE**   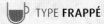 TYPE **FRAPPÉ**   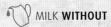 MILK **WITHOUT**

The pectin in the pear and apple is a natural thickener, and it is surprising how frothy this frappé becomes after a little blending. Rosewater subtly suggests sweetness, while quercetin in the fibrous fruit skins boosts immunity.

1 **pear**, cored and sliced, with skin on

1 **apple**, cored and sliced, with skin on

1 tsp **lemon zest**

1½ tsp **rosewater**

10 **ice cubes**

Special equipment
blender

1 Place the pear and apple slices, lemon zest, and rosewater in a blender. Pour over 240ml (8fl oz) water and blend until smooth.

2 Add the ice cubes into the blender and blend just until the ice has crushed.

SERVE IT UP Pour into 2 tumblers and serve immediately.

SPICY SWEET ROOIBOS SERVES 2

 TEMP **100°C (210°F)**   INFUSE **5 MINS**   TYPE **FRAPPÉ**   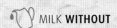 MILK **WITHOUT**

Drink fresh fruit frappés right away as they start to darken quickly. Cardamom aids digestion, helps detox, and is a cold remedy. It also imparts a fragrant spice perfume to the sweet peach.

1 heaped tbsp **rooibos leaves**

500ml (16fl oz) boiling **water**

2 **ripe or canned peaches**, cored and sliced

½ tsp **cardamom powder**

3 tsp **honey**

5 **ice cubes**

Special equipment
blender

1 Place the rooibos leaves in a teapot, add the boiling water, and leave to infuse for 5 minutes. Then strain the infusion and set aside to cool.

2 Place the peach, cardamom powder, and honey in a blender. Pour over the cooled infusion and blend until smooth.

3 Add the ice cubes and blend until frothy.

SERVE IT UP Pour into 2 tumblers and serve immediately.

FRUITY SPICY FRAGRANT

COOL TROPICS FLOAT SERVES 2

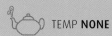 TEMP **NONE**   INFUSE **NONE**   TYPE **FLOAT**   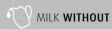 MILK **WITHOUT**

A cross between a smoothie and a float, this is a fun drink for dessert. Mint's natural tonic qualities enliven the blend, but the yogurt floating on top and splashing around in the ginger bubbles is the highlight.

1 **kiwi**, peeled and chopped

5 large **mint leaves**, plus 2 small sprigs, to garnish

65g (2¼oz) **pineapple**, diced

2 large scoops **frozen vanilla yogurt**

240ml (8fl oz) **ginger beer** or **ginger ale**

Special equipment
blender

1 Place the kiwi, mint, pineapple, and 120ml (4fl oz) water in the blender, then blend until smooth.

2 Pour this mixture into 2 tumblers, and add a scoop of the frozen yogurt to each.

SERVE IT UP Top up with ginger beer, garnish with mint, and serve with a straw.

MINT SMOOTHIE SERVES 2

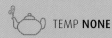 TEMP **NONE**   INFUSE **NONE**    TYPE **SMOOTHIE**    MILK **ALMOND**

Use spearmint leaves as all other mints will pale in comparison. The avocado lends a mellow creaminess to the smoothie. Even with water and almond milk, you almost need to eat this with a spoon.

½ **avocado**, flesh scooped out

¼ **cucumber**, peeled, deseeded, and diced

2 tbsp **chopped spearmint leaves**

175ml (6fl oz) **sweetened almond milk**

Special equipment
blender

1 Place the avocado, cucumber, and spearmint in the blender.

2 Pour 175ml (6fl oz) water and the almond milk into the blender, and blend for about 1 minute until smooth.

SERVE IT UP Pour the smoothie into 2 tumblers.

MINTY CREAMY GREEN

Cool Tropics Float The interplay of ginger beer and yogurt makes this an effervescent drink.

ALOE THERE FRAPPÉ! SERVES 2

 TEMP **NONE**   INFUSE **NONE**    TYPE **FRAPPÉ**    MILK **WITHOUT**

It may seem odd to pair a sweet fruit with a herb, but basil's mint and liquorice notes go really well with strawberries. Be prepared to be pleasantly surprised as aloe juice makes for a very frothy frappé.

10 **strawberries**, sliced

2 tbsp **chopped basil leaves**

240ml (8fl oz) **aloe juice**

4 **ice cubes**

Special equipment
blender

1 Place the strawberries, basil leaves, and aloe juice in a blender and blend until smooth and frothy. The heavy froth is a result of the gel in the aloe juice.

2 Add the ice cubes and continue to blend until the ice has crushed.

SERVE IT UP Pour into 2 tumblers.

MAYAN SUNSET SERVES 2

 TEMP **NONE**   INFUSE **NONE**    TYPE **SMOOTHIE**   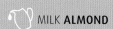 MILK **ALMOND**

This fun and flavourful drink can be adapted to individual tastes by simply playing with the level of sweetness. If you are feeling adventurous, build the heat with a little cayenne pepper.

2 tbsp **unsweetened cocoa powder**

¼ tsp **ground cinnamon**

1 tsp **chilli powder**

3 tbsp **honey**

150g (5½oz) or half a block of **silken tofu**, diced

350ml (12fl oz) **almond milk**

Special equipment
blender

1 Place the cocoa, cinnamon, and chilli powder in a blender. Add the honey, tofu, and almond milk.

2 Blend until the mixture is smooth and creamy.

SERVE IT UP Pour into 2 tumblers.

CREAM SPICY CHOCOLATE

COCONUT KAFFIR FLOAT SERVES 2

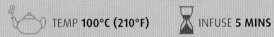 TEMP **100°C (210°F)**   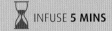 INFUSE **5 MINS**   TYPE **FLOAT**    MILK **COCONUT ICE CREAM**

Fragrant and exotic, this fizzy concoction tastes like something you might drink on a tropical island. The citrussy flavour of the kaffir lime leaves cuts beautifully through the creaminess of the coconut ice cream.

8 tbsp **torn kaffir lime leaves**

generous pinch of **lavender buds**

240ml (8fl oz) boiling **water**

2 large scoops **coconut ice cream**

240ml (8fl oz) **chilled soda water**

1 Place the lime leaves and the lavender buds in a teapot, add the boiling water, and leave to infuse for 5 minutes.

2 Strain the infusion and pour into a glass jug. Leave to cool and then chill for 1 hour.

SERVE IT UP Place 1 scoop of coconut ice cream in each tumbler and pour over the infusion. Stir gently, add the chilled soda water, and serve.

SUNNY MANGO SMOOTHIE SERVES 2

 TEMP **NONE**   INFUSE **NONE**    TYPE **SMOOTHIE**    MILK **ALMOND**

This drink gets its mellow yellow glow from curcumin, the substance that gives turmeric root its bright yellow colour. Rich in antioxidants, it combines with mango and yogurt to make a creamy and sweet smoothie.

1 **mango**, cut into slices

1 tsp **grated turmeric root**, or
  ½ tsp **turmeric powder**

150ml (5fl oz) **plain low-fat yogurt**

1 tsp **honey**

300ml (10fl oz) **sweetened almond milk**

Special equipment
blender

1 Place the mango, turmeric, yogurt, and honey in a blender and blend for a few seconds.

2 Add the almond milk into the blender and blend until completely smooth and creamy.

SERVE IT UP Pour the smoothie into 2 tumblers.

GLOSSARY

ASTRINGENT A sensation of the texture of tea's **liquor**, which causes tissues in the mouth to contract.

Ayurveda A system of traditional Hindu medicine using plant-based treatments.

AUTUMNAL Describes leaves picked late in the harvest (September–October), noted for their mellow flavours.

BODY The overall depth of flavour often associated with black tea.

BRICK TEA A compressed tea cake, made by pressing steamed tea leaves into the shape of a brick.

BRIGHT A description of flavour in black tea, usually characterized by a mild astringency and fresh flavour.

BRISK A tasting term to describe a lively, slightly astringent sensation. Usually associated with black tea, especially Ceylon.

CAFFEINE A naturally occurring chemical stimulant. It is produced in young leaf buds to protect them from insects.

CAMELLIA SINENSIS An evergreen shrub whose leaves and leaf buds are used to produce tea. There are two varieties: var. *sinensis* and var. *assamica.*

CATECHINS A type of polyphenol and powerful antioxidant found in tea that helps to stabilize free radicals (cells that are damaged by environmental pollution).

CHANOYU An elaborate and formal Japanese tea ceremony, which dictates certain movements, procedures, and equipment to be used for the making and serving of Matcha tea.

CHASEN A small whisk constructed of a single piece of bamboo that has been sliced into fine tines, and is used to whisk Matcha with water.

CHAWAN A sturdy ceramic-footed bowl used to prepare Matcha. It is used in the Japanese **Chanoyu** ceremony.

CULTIVARS A cultivated variety of plant intentionally bred with particular flavour or growing attributes.

DECOCTION A preparation made by boiling herbs in water.

FLUSH The growth of new buds on the tea bush that occurs several times during the plucking/harvesting season.

GAIWAN A Chinese lidded bowl with saucer, usually made of porcelain or glass. It is used to make small quantities of tea for tasting.

GRADE A method used in Sri Lanka, Kenya, and India to determine the quality of the dry leaf based on appearance alone.

INFUSION The liquid tea made by soaking tea leaves in hot (or sometimes cold) water.

KILL GREEN The process of steaming or **pan-firing** tea leaves that will be used for green tea. This prevents the leaves from oxidizing.

L THEANINE A unique amino acid found in tea, which can reduce stress and induce a sense of well-being.

LIQUOR The strained tea liquid created from infusing tea leaves in hot water.

MOUTHFEEL A description of the physical sensation of drinking tea, such as soft, astringent, or creamy.

NOSE The aroma of the **liquor**.

ORTHODOX A method of production of tea that aims to keep the tea leaf as whole as possible.

OXIDATION The process of the (partial or complete) chemical breakdown of enzymes in tea leaves upon exposure to oxygen and heat.

PAN-FIRED Refers to green tea leaves that have been stirred in a wok pan to dry them or "kill green".

PEKOE (pronounced peck–o) The fine hairs on new tea buds. Also a term used in the British grading system indicating a fine grade of tea.

POLYPHENOLS Antioxidants that help detox the body. Tea has around eight times more polyphenols than fruits or vegetables.

PU'ER A dark tea from China's Yunnan province with probiotic content that develops as the tea ages. Is available in loose leaf or cake form.

TISANE A herbal infusion made from the leaves, roots, seeds, fruit, flowers, or bark of plants.

TERROIR The particular conditions in which tea is grown.

UMAMI A Japanese term for savoury flavour, which is found in many steamed Japanese green teas.

VOLATILE OILS The aromatic oils in tea leaves that will evaporate on exposure to heat and oxygen.

YIXING A region in Jiangsu province, China, where a dark purple clay is used to create unglazed tea pots using a hand building technique. These are called Yixing pots.

INDEX

Page numbers in **bold** indicate recipes.

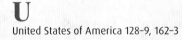

ABOUT THE AUTHOR

Linda Gaylard is a Canadian Tea Sommelier, certified by The Tea Association of Canada and a graduate of the Tea Sommelier programme from the culinary arts facility of George Brown College in Toronto. In 2009, she left a career as an influential wardrobe stylist to launch the website The Tea Stylist, for which she is best known. Linda also writes for international tea publications, appears in television interviews and on lifestyle video blogs, and hosts tea tastings and events.

On her quest for tea knowledge, Linda has travelled around the world, including to China and Korea, where she has toured farms, met producers, and tasted exquisite teas. Linda regularly attends and gives talks at tea fairs around the world, including the World Tea Expo.

ACKNOWLEDGMENTS

The author would like to acknowledge the encouragement of her friends and family (especially Angus, Malcolm, and Roger), and the generosity of her colleagues in the tea industry – a community that is eager to share knowledge and celebrate one's achievements. Thank you also to Kathy Woolley, DK's Project Editor who kept us all on course. I raise a cuppa to you all!

DK would like to extend warm thanks to Don Mei and Celine Thiry of Chinalifetea.com for the Chinese Gongfu Cha, Peter Cavaciuti, Michi Warren, and Teiko Sugie of the Kaetsu Chado Society for the Japanese Chanoyu, and Jeunghyun Choi for the Korean Darye.

They would also like to thank:
Photography: William Reavell
Home economist: Jane Lawrie
Prop styling: Isabel de Cordova
Proofreading: Claire Cross
Indexing: Vanessa Bird
Editorial assistance: Bob Bridle
Design assistance: Laura Buscemi
Cartographic assistance: Simon Mumford

Picture credits
The publisher would like to thanks the following for their kind permission to reproduce their photographs:

(Key: a–above; b–below/bottom; c–centre; f–far; l–left; r–right; t–top)

14(b) Linda Gaylard, **66**(tc) Linda Gaylard, **91**(tr) Christopher Pillitz © Dorling Kindersley, **119**(br) Barnabas Kindersley © Dorling Kindersley, **128–129**(bc) Linda Gaylard, **136**(cl) Mark Winwood © Dorling Kindersley, Courtesy of RHS Wisley.

All other images © Dorling Kindersley.

A NOTE ON THE MAPS
Tea leaf icons represent the location of notable tea-producing regions on pp74–129. Green shading indicates tea production in a larger area over approximate climate-driven geographical areas.